PLAY
IN A PEACE
PROCESS

DAVE DUGGAN

GUILDHALL PRESS

First published in June 2008 by
Guildhall Press
Unit 15
Ráth Mór Business Park
Bligh's Lane
Derry
Northern Ireland
BT48 0LZ
T: (028) 7136 4413 F: (028) 7137 2949
info@ghpress.com www.ghpress.com

ISBN 978 1 906271 13 8

We gratefully acknowledge the financial support of the Arts Council of
Northern Ireland under its Multi-Annual Lottery Programme.

A CIP record for this book is available from the British Library.

Reproduction and Performance Caution

About the Author

Dave Duggan is a writer and director living in Derry. Between 1996 and 2007, he wrote and directed plays and sketches for Sole Purpose Productions which is the work included in this book, *Plays in a Peace Process*.

Waiting.... has been seen in New York, Liverpool and at the Edinburgh Fringe, as well as in Ireland. The *British Theatre Guide* commented that, 'Dave Duggan has been nominated for an Oscar and from the quality of his writing in this edgy political drama, one can see why.'

AH 6905 was used by Dah Teatar Belgrade in their latest production, and an adaptation and production of the play took place in Kabul, Afghanistan, in early 2008.

Dave's other work includes *Spike Dreams*, a Derry Playhouse production, which toured Ireland in 2003. *Bubbles in the Hot Tub*, a comedy for Blue Eagle Productions, opened in the Millennium Forum, Derry, and toured regionally in early 2007. His stage play in Irish – *Gruagairí*, for Aisling Ghéar – opened in Belfast and toured nationally in the autumn of 2007. He was awarded the 2007 Stewart Parker Trust / BBC Award for writing in Irish.

His radio drama credits include *The Man with No Ears*, *The Blackbird's Last Campaign*, *Scenes from an Inquiry*, *Joe s'Againne* and *Painting the Loft* for RTÉ Radio 1, and *From a Great Height* for BBC Radio 4, described by the *Daily Telegraph* as a 'funny, odd, touching, original play'.

Dave has written a number of original screenplays for short films for Raw Nerve Productions, including *Cú Chulainn* and the Oscar / Academy Award-nominated *Dance Lexie Dance*. He wrote and directed a short film called *Tumble Turns* for Raw Nerve.

Lagan Press published his *Shorts for Stage and Screen*. Guildhall Press published his novel *The Greening of Larry Mahon*, which *The Guardian* described as 'an engrossing study of shifting rootlessness'.

Contents

These plays and sketches may be read in the order in which they were produced.

The Shopper and the Boy (1996)

Without the Walls (1998)

Waiting.... (2000)

Scenes from an Inquiry (2002)

The Saville Inquiry London Scenarios (2002)

It's Only a Brick (2003)

The Recruiting Office (2004)

AH 6905 (2005)

A Kick in the Stomach and A Kick in the Teeth (2006)

The Anti-Sectarianism Cabaret (2006)

Riders to the Road (2007)

Foreword

'Art should cause violence to be set aside.
And it is only art that can accomplish this.'
Leo Tolstoy

A protracted period of historical conflict between Britain and Ireland erupted in violence, centred on Northern Ireland, in 1968. Moves towards peace began in 1994, culminating in political agreements that led to a locally elected legislative assembly. *Plays in a Peace Process* brings together seven plays and four sketches I wrote between 1996 and 2007 as a contribution to this Peace Process. I wrote other plays, films, radio drama and a novel, but the works in this book are the core of my artistic work in that period, because, like all my fellow citizens, I was living through the Peace Process, and writing is what I do. This work was professionally produced and toured, nationally and internationally, by Sole Purpose Productions. I am indebted to Patricia Byrne, in particular, and to the many actors, producers, designers, musicians and technicians who ensured these works were realised, while often taking considerable personal risks.

Imagine a room in the Indian Cultural Centre in Belfast. The set for the play *Waiting....* – a bus stop with a bench – is in place. Myself, as writer and director, and the two actors make final preparations before our audience arrives. In a corner of the room is a beautiful large-scale representation of the Hindu elephant god, Ganesh, Remover of Obstacles and Patron of Arts and Sciences. We smile gently to ourselves as we talk about a phrase that had become common in those years. 'The elephant in the room' refers to problems that cannot be faced, that cannot be spoken about: sectarianism, cultural stand-offs, the impact of violence by the state or by paramilitaries, collusion by police officers with paramilitaries, the search for truth. So many elephants in so many rooms.

The play starts. A political ex-prisoner meets the husband of a woman she blew up. The audience, drawn from unionist and nationalist communities, watch intently, under the benevolent gaze of Ganesh, as obstacles to discussion and engagement between a victim and perpetrator of violence are removed – as peace is built.

The plays and the sketches in this book did not arise from processes of analysis and reflection. Rather the press of public events as they happened drew them out of me. The plays grew out of pressures on my sensibilities, pressures that led me to respond artistically, to find forms that could contain the impulses to make theatre, to find language that could give voice to those pressures, to create characters that would make manifest my responses to the Peace Process occurring in my society through that time.

Because the main resource I bring to bear at all times in my work is imagination, and because theatre is a visual medium, I ask you to imagine once more: a small church hall at the edge of the village of Kesh on the Fermanagh–Donegal border, in the north-west of Ireland. The local Community Development Association is hosting a performance of *The Shopper and the Boy*. It is a glorious June evening. Standing outside the hall, we hear larks singing high in the summer air. A machine is cutting grass for silage two fields away. Preparations for the performance are made, but the local hosts are worried. Earlier that day, the remains of an RUC police officer shot dead in Lurgan were returned to his family home near the village. There is a quietness about the people. Some think it would be a bad idea to go ahead with the play. Some think no one will turn up. Some say we should go ahead, that the play, which dramatises the difficult issue of loyalist marching, needs to be seen. I wait with the actors, saying we'll perform or not as the Community Association decides.

Gradually a large audience starts to gather – from the village, the surrounding area and across the border in

Donegal. There are brief nods of recognition, some easy greetings, polite acknowledgements, a delicate tension. The crowd is muted, diffident, but ready to see the play. The Community Association decides to proceed. The actors prepare. The set is in place. The play begins. The actors appear and march with a trunk around the space. The Boy steps forward, faces the audience and declaims, 'No surrender!' The Shopper steps forward and declaims, 'Tiocfaidh ár lá!' The audience sits forward and engages. There is space, time and a focus to face the elephant in the room.

An audience sees real people close up, grappling with painful and difficult matters, with resolve and imagination, in poetic characters who are mirrors of themselves. The truth, that questions can be more important than answers, is laid out. Poetic, intelligent language in the mouths of ordinary people offers possibilities. The Shopper and the Boy express their contending desires as manifestations of nascent negotiations. Negotiations need space, and theatre has given a public this space, shown instances of the space being used, shown negotiations occurring on the basis of respect, not mere tolerance.

This can be seen as part of the processes in peace-building described by Azar, Burton and others as Track 2 Diplomacy, unofficial processes at public and community levels that parallel formal political diplomacy. These are necessary because, as George Bernard Shaw said, 'Social questions never get solved until the pressure becomes so desperate that even governments recognise the necessity for moving. And to bring the pressure to this point, the poets must lend a hand to the few willing to do public work in stages at which nothing but abuse is to be gained by it.'

Imagine yet again: a working-class housing estate in Newtownards, a town just east of Belfast, with a perceived unionist population. My play *Without the Walls* is in the form of a Greek tragedy, drawing on the Antigone story, using rhyme and masks to dramatise the question of how a society moving out of conflict might police itself. An audience is engaged by an act of debate, education and entertainment, and when the tragedy is delivered and the woman is dead, two women sitting near me have tears running down their cheeks. Moments of catharsis in theatre prepare us for moments of resolve in the world; in this instance, strengthening ourselves to face the changes that a new policing order will bring.

By the year 2000 the Peace Process was well underway, stuttering and staggering as the political process moved and stalled at different points. I have always taken the view that the Peace Process is a continuous thing. Not something that started in the early 1990s with the Hume–Adams dialogues and the ceasefires. The Peace Process continues for as long as the violence is manifest. People in different ways seek to move things on by non-violent means, trying to keep avenues of dialogue open, striving to maintain contacts, advancing actions for the securing of human rights and dignity. By the end of the 1990s the phrase 'moving on' was being used by politicians and other public figures in Britain and Ireland. The notion of our society being in a post-conflict situation was in the public domain. Prisoner releases were happening. Demands were being made of victims and perpetrators of violence to turn away from the past and to face the future. I wondered how individuals, deeply affected by the conflict, through loss or imprisonment, might actually address, in real terms, the need to move on.

Imagine a hushed audience in the wonderful studio space of The Market Place Theatre in the beautiful city of Armagh. In my absurdist version of the meeting between a bomber and a victim in the play *Waiting....*, the gravity of this meeting, the searing import of what could be a real meeting on the streets of that city or any city, town or village in Northern Ireland, stills the audience. The two characters struggle to articulate their experiences in words I wrote to impress hope on the world. Hope, but not sentimentality.

9

Theatre has given that audience a collective experience that will support the private and public processes that must happen when individuals and societies do indeed move on in a meaningful way. For that audience and for us all, the challenge remains to live as fully as possible in the present, with the past, and for the future. It is one of the powerful qualities of theatre that Arthur Miller says it is 'the art of the present tense', and being with characters as they wrestle with the reality of moving on in a society coming out of conflict provides a collective experience that strengthens us all and contributes to the Peace Process.

I recall a performance of *Waiting....* in a small theatre in New York in 2002. I was standing in the wings, watching the two actors go through the familiar moves, reciting the familiar lines. And as I listened to the audience laughing at the absurd opening dialogue and then settle into quiet attention as the characters revealed more and more of their lives, pain and hopes, I knew that once again theatre was providing a collective experience that augmented the lives of the people in that theatre, that city, and in a small way was contributing to peace-building in the face of awful violence and vengeful public language.

One of the significant complications in the Peace Process in Northern Ireland is the fact that the state is a protagonist and a perpetrator of violence. The Saville Inquiry into the events of Bloody Sunday in 1972, when fourteen people were killed by state forces on the streets of Derry Londonderry, is still continuing. The way the Saville Inquiry proceeded had a profound impact on me. I found myself sitting in the public gallery transfixed by the witnesses and their stories, the dry language of the legal teams, the formal discourse of the judges and the layout of the room. It was self-evidently theatre to me and I felt the impulse to poeticise the activity of the Inquiry, to elevate the language of the testimonies and the questioning so that something of the greater human experience might be made public.

I wrote *Scenes from an Inquiry* with the support and participation of the Bloody Sunday Families. I later did a radio drama adaptation at the request of RTÉ through which the public poetry of the imagined witnesses reached a national audience in Ireland. It was the power of poetry I was seeking – the universal poetic voice that cries out in the face of awful violence, that salves and heals in the face of the utter hopelessness of death and loss.

In this way, a piece of theatre has offered healing of great pain, has acted as a balm to wounded hearts and minds. It has assisted in the breaking of taboos by offering some people a different view of the world. A unionist member of the Policing Board attended a performance and spoke to me afterwards saying he enjoyed it and found it thought-provoking.

Family members spoke of the truth of it. That's the ironic thing. A work of fiction and imagination evokes a sense of truth. Something of the power of the unashamed subjectivity of theatre is evident here: the way theatre deals with feelings and experiences and, in this case, poeticises them, so that it makes a contribution to the Peace Process as an agent of healing and truth seeking.

In the final analysis, the plays are entertainment. Going to see one is a good night out, a guarantee of a good time, in a wide-ranging sense of that phrase. And with violence still a fact of life on the streets amidst a stuttering political process, entertainment is an important contribution theatre makes towards peace-building. The very existence of such plays indicates what Bertolt Brecht described as, 'A powerful social movement which has an interest in free discussion of vital problems, the better to solve them, and which can defend this interest against all opposing tendencies.'

As the Peace Process bedded down and politics started to take over from violence in the early twenty-first century in Ireland, social and economic problems came to the fore, still in the context of a society coming out of conflict.

Where will the jobs come from and on what conditions will we gain employment? What hopelessness drives our young adults to recklessness and death on our roads? I continued to write plays, because of the need for a place where such matters could be put under sustained artistic scrutiny.

These plays and sketches work as art in the first instance. They are not acts of politics or social work in the direct sense of those words. They are instances of the application of imagination to public events, attempts to find beauty and order amidst chaos and present them to audiences who will make up their own minds about them. And when it works, as director John McGrath said, 'We come out feeling exhilarated: we are more alive for seeing it, more aware of the possibilities of the human race, more fully human ourselves.' In the face of the extreme violence – great public tensions, traumatic separation of people, betrayal, subjugation and loss – that occurred in Northern Ireland, theatre penetrated into the darkest zones of terror and despair and made light present in the darkness.

That theatre could contribute to peace-building should not surprise us. After all, conflict is at the heart of good drama. We may in fact be seeing an example of what peace researcher Johann Galtung means when he talks about conflict as positive and negative energy, vying and contending across the realms of human endeavour. Theatre offers conflict as positive energy and as American dramatist David Mamet asserts, 'What you and I want from art is peace.'

Peace can only be built if we give attention to our irrationality, give attention to the deepest, often most troubling, urges and impulses that make us human. In so far as politics engages with power, art and, in particular, theatre, engages with pleasure, so that while facts may be disputed, fictions can be enjoyed, relished and savoured, used to bring truth to bear and thus build peace. Theatre work like this, in a variety of forms, both tragic and comic, is happening all over the world in places where peace processes run in parallel with war processes.

As current events slowly become history in Ireland, these plays exist as a contribution to peace-building internationally. They now exist in the wider world in support of such efforts. I gave permission to theatre-makers in Kabul, Afghanistan, to adapt and translate my play *AH 6905*. They reported to me that the performances, first in Dari and later in Pashtun, took place in early 2008 in the ruins of the Russian Cultural Centre, a legacy of a past conflict.

During the performance, echoes from life outside could be heard through ripped-out walls and holes caused by projectiles: a policeman's walkie-talkie, the siren of an ambulance, a kids' quarrel, and the continuous hum of a concrete mixer, for in Kabul building goes on everywhere. And when the performance was over, a sudden gust of wind ripped away the fabric that was covering the holes in the walls, and, together with clouds of dust, daylight forced its way in.

Dave Duggan
June 2008

And now, History and Time have stopped,
as if they were cogs in a great engine
turning the century and I stuck my little
finger in there. So they're stopped.

Production Details 1

The three plays in this section – *Waiting....*, *The Shopper and the Boy*, and *Without the Walls* – show characters striving to negotiate their way out of difficulties as the Peace Process got stuck on issues to do with prisoner releases, loyalist marches and changes to policing. Intimidation was, and is, a problem, and the sketch *It's Only a Brick* was commissioned for a conference dealing with that issue.

Waiting.... was first produced by Sole Purpose Productions at The Playhouse, Derry Londonderry, on 4 February 2000. The director was Dave Duggan, set design was by Jan Vaclav Caspers, set construction by Jim Keys, and the company was Patricia Byrne and Jonathan Burgess. I acknowledge the influence of Samuel Beckett's *Waiting for Godot* in this dramatisation of the meeting at a bus stop between a victim and a perpetrator of political violence.

The Shopper and the Boy was first produced by Sole Purpose Productions at Foyle Arts Centre, Derry Londonderry, on 20 June 1996. The director was Dave Duggan, the set designer was Jan Vaclav Caspers, and the company was Patricia Byrne and Darren Greer. It dramatises the cultural and physical clashes between a loyalist Apprentice Boy and a nationalist mother. The last speech echoes Bertolt Brecht's play *The Good Person of Szechwan*.

Without the Walls was first produced by Sole Purpose Productions at Foyle Arts Centre, Derry Londonderry, on 16 March 1998. The director was Dave Duggan, the set designer was Jan Vaclav Caspers, set construction was by Jim Keys, and the company was Patricia Byrne, Jonathan Burgess and Jim Keys. I acknowledge the influence of Sophocles' play *Antigone* in this dramatisation of the challenge of policing when the state is changing due to political conflict.

*It's **Only a Brick*** was first produced, under commission from WAVE, by Sole Purpose Productions at Cullybackey, County Antrim, on 1 October 2003 for a conference on intimidation. The director was Dave Duggan and the company was Patricia Byrne and Dave Duggan.

Waiting....

A pole with a bench seat. It could be a bus stop. Morning.

There is a pair of dice on the bench, snake eyes showing. At different times, the characters play with them, especially in pauses marked 'Time passes'.

A woman enters carrying a suitcase. She plays dice. She sits. Time passes.

A man enters. They play dice. He stands and looks right. Time passes.

Man No sign? (*Time passes.*) They shouldn't victimise us like this, you know.

Woman No sign yet. But that's hardly surprising.

Man You're new. I mean, I haven't seen you here before. But you seem to know about it.

Woman Oh! I know about it. I've served my time. I've done my share of waiting. I've done what I could to pass the time.

Man Me, too.

Time passes.

Man I often play games. To pass the time. Usually with myself. No one else to play them with now. Oh! When we were young. First married (*Animated.*), we had so many games. So many games. Do you know the one... "I went on holidays"? It goes... I went on holidays and I brought... an apple. Then you say, 'I went on holidays and I brought an apple and a... a... brush.' Then I do the letter c. The list gets longer...

Woman I haven't been on holiday for a long time. Since I was a wean really. Some people say I should go on one now. But I'm not so sure...

Man That doesn't matter. It's just a game. It will pass the time.

Woman If you like.

Man I went on holiday and I brought an apple. Now your go. The letter b.

Woman I went on holiday and I brought an apple. And a bomb.

Man I went on holiday and I brought an apple. A bomb. And a car.

Woman I went on holiday and I brought an apple. A bomb. A car. And a detonator.

Man I went on holiday and I brought an apple. A bomb. A car. A detonator. The list gets longer. And an elephant.

Woman Why did you bring an elephant?

Man Why did you bring a bomb?

Woman It's not a game.

Man It's not a game.

Time passes.

Woman Do you think we'll ever really have a holiday? People like us.

Man People like us! You say it as if we were the same. As if we were friends. How could we be friends? We can't even play a simple game together.

Woman A real holiday. Somewhere foreign. With sun.

Man Have to be foreign for sun.

Woman And a beach with palm trees and white surf, curling, curling...

Man And a small bar, thatch-covered, and a grinning man serving cold beer and peanuts and the two of us sitting on rattan couches in the shade watching the white surf curling, curling...

Woman We've never been there. I have no memory of that.

Man We have. We have. It was our honeymoon. Not us, I mean. Yes, I have a memory of that.

Woman Tell me. It will pass the time.

Man The grinning man was called Carl and as soon as we'd approach he'd crack open two cold beers – arctic cold – and I'd say, 'Have one yourself, Carl,' and he'd crack another open and the three of us would clink bottles together and we'd all grin. Then we'd sit under the shade on the rattan couch, big enough for two, and you'd lay back so that the living breathing sculpture of your body would stun me. Oh! I have a memory of that.

Man *sits.* **Woman** *makes as if she would approach him but doesn't.*

Time passes.

Man You didn't answer my question.

Woman Which one?

Man Why did you bring a bomb?

Woman Let me just say there is... was... a war on.

Man I know. She was my war baby. (*Sings.*) Baby, Baby, Baby, Baby, Oh, Baby, I love you. I really do. (*Speaks.*) Karen Carpenter. We loved her. The Carpenters. Came to a sad end. Like so many. A sad end. You said you served your time. You went to prison?

Woman That's why you haven't seen me before. I'm just out.

Woman *looks left and right then paces up and down.*

Woman I kept moving. Got to keep moving. Cover those wings. I kept fit. I worked out. Mr Motivator on TV.

Man You watched television?

Woman Of course. I was in prison. Not in hell. Though some people said I should have been. But it doesn't matter. Not television. Not work-outs. Not educational courses. Not drama classes. Not anything except time passing. Time passing.

Man Why did you do it?

Woman I... like I said. We were at war. You act first, reflect afterwards. It's the natural order.

Man I don't watch television. Not since... Television. TV. Too Violent. We used to watch it. Had our own favourite programmes. We liked Blind Date. (*Liverpool accent.*) A lorra lorra laffs and a lorra lorra fun. All right, Chuck. We could play it now. You and me. We need a screen. Doesn't matter. We can close our eyes. We're good at that. Closing our eyes. Not seeing things. Right. You sit – you need a rest. I'll ask the questions. Then you can see if you like me.

Woman Friendship by interrogation. I don't have good experiences of that.

Man We're not talking about friendship. There's too big a screen between us for that. This is not a date. We're not blind. How could we possibly play?

Time passes.

Man We're not to be friends. We're not the same. We could never be. You're still alive.

Woman So are you.

Man All we can do is live. Born across a bomb crater, eh?

Woman All we can do is live. Play the game of life. Yes. I agree with that. But we're still left with the question of how we live. Is it to be free and equal? Or second class in our own country?

Man Like I said, you are alive. And you can just go on and on like that if you want. You probably got an Open

23

University degree when you were in prison. Did a bit of thinking. But none of that changes one thing. You're alive and she's dead.

Woman Look, I didn't ask for this. You want games. I'll give you games.

She pulls a deck of cards out of her pocket and starts dealing two hands onto the ground in front of her.

Five card. Here, two hands. There. Look at that. Aces there. Not even a pair here. It depends on the hand you're dealt. You've got to play the cards you're dealt. Look at that. Another ace. Who said the deck's not stacked?

Man *picks up a hand.*

Man I haven't played cards in years. There was always a deck on the mantelpiece in my granny's house. Near the round-faced clock. We only played when there was a power cut. Granny played patience by candle light.

Woman Did your granny play poker? Five card?

Man My granny never gambled.

Woman She got up every morning of every day she could, didn't she? That's a gamble.

Man You were right. This is not a game.

He throws the cards down. She gathers the deck up and puts it in her pocket.

Time passes.

Man Life is not a game of chance.

Woman No, you're right. It's more a system of rules. Checks and balances. Urges and regulations. And we all have to make our own way in it. Sometimes it comes down to where you were born. Here, look. Now here's a game for you.

She takes a game of Monopoly out of her suitcase and sets it up on the bench.

Which piece do you want? The top hat? The car? The ship? Got to keep moving. Chance cards. Go to jail. Move directly to jail. Do not pass 'go'. Do not collect two hundred pound. A throw of the dice determines what street you grew up on. (*Throws dice.*) Falls. Shankill. Waterside. Bogside. Mayfair. Park Lane. Now we're talking. Some people did all right out of it. You don't have a monopoly on suffering, you know.

Man And you don't have a monopoly on history. Or time. Or the future.

Woman So what do we do now? Knock it all down and build town houses on it? Stick up a load of hotels so the tourists can come and see us play?

Man It's not a game.

He closes over the Monopoly board.

Woman It never was.

She packs the game away.

Time passes.

Man I've lost my being. My vital organs. People pass me in the town and say, 'That's your man whose wife was blown up.' That's who I am now. The media vultures contact me at anniversaries. Or for comment when some other poor victim is being lined up for the cameras. 'And what do you think?' Think! How can anyone 'think'?

Woman It's not your fault. You mustn't blame yourself. History picked on you. It was in the cards. Life is a gamble.

Man That's not good enough. I know what you mean. But it's not good enough. She was stolen from me. We were burgled ourselves once. (*Laughs.*) In our sleep. They took the lot. TV. Video. Credit cards. My glasses. What use were they going to make of them? Snoring away upstairs, the two of us. When we got the police they were civil and offered little hope. Apparently thieves are so efficient nowadays, they've already got the market organised before they steal anything. Perhaps they'd found someone wanting to buy reading glasses. That might explain it. I felt so impotent, so powerless. So ravaged. Standing there in my own kitchen, looking at the back-door lock they'd forced, so gently and so thoroughly. Through which they'd thieved our purses, our video, our TV and my glasses. As if they'd pulled the eyes out of my head. Then a policewoman with a kindly smile said, 'That's all for now. We'll be in touch if we have any news.' Her eyes told me she didn't expect to have any news. Then she handed me a leaflet and left, saying, 'You might find this helpful.' I glanced down at it and read the word 'victim' and I folded it into a tiny square and threw it onto the worktop.

I came upon it again, weeks later, after the bombing. I've only just remembered how close the two incidents were. That's good. It's marvellous how conversation helps memory. It was still there on the worktop, behind the bread bin, slightly opened out and grimy. I unfolded the squares and spread the leaflet out. I read the word 'victim' once more and I felt the anger well up inside me. This is not the word for me. I am not a victim. I am not to be pitied. I took that leaflet and I tore it and ripped it into tiny, tiny shreds. Shreds. They made shreds of her. I didn't need pity. I needed assistance. What use is pity when you're planning revenge. I wanted revenge. I simply wanted to meet someone who did it and gouge their eyes out.

Woman Was anyone arrested for…

Man Yes. Two of them. They had a string of burglaries behind them, but they could only make the charges stick on one. The other got off.

Woman One was damned and one was saved.

Man Luke 23:43. You know your Bible. I suppose you read that, too.

Woman I've had plenty of time for reading over the years.

Man The penitent thief. And Jesus said, 'Verily I say onto thee, today thou shalt be with me in Paradise.' Aye. Paradise. With a barman called Carl, serving cold beer and the surf curling, curling in, and two sets of footprints in the sand. Two sets. Then one. One set. Alone.

Woman Do you still want revenge? Are you still angry?

Man Naw. You know… time… passes. It's as if I've had a major operation and had a big vital organ cut out of me, but I've lived on. Survived. Most days I wish I hadn't.

Don't laugh. But some days I wish I'd been shredded, too. Like the leaflet. But I'm still whole. Almost. Walking around with the word VICTIM stamped all over me. It's hopeless.

Woman It can't be. Even at my lowest, I felt hope flicker. Had to keep that flicker going. Arrest, interrogation, remand, interrogation, remand, trial, conviction. Sentence. The long wait. You prepare yourself. It's part of the deal. You don't do what I did unless you're prepared to do the time. But actually doing it. Life. Nothing but time passing. And damning yourself. Judgement. That's the worst of it. Your own judgement.

Man But you were alive. You are here now.

Woman I know. In some ways that's the hard part. Having a life to rebuild.

Man It's a legacy. Like something bequeathed to us. This has happened and you are left this way because of it. And there is no way of rolling back the great stone. No turning back of the clock.

Woman Is something coming?

Man *looks and shakes his head.*

Time passes.

Man What was it like, in prison? Did they interrogate you?

Woman At the time of arrest, yes. All the time. Who was with you? Where's the stuff? Do you know so and so? When did you dye your hair? That's you on the screen there, isn't it?

Man Twenty questions.

Woman What?

Man Twenty questions.

Woman At least.

Man No. I mean... it's twenty questions. I think of something – no, I can't think of anything any more, not really – you think of something and I ask you questions and you only answer 'yes' or 'no' and you win if I don't find out what you're thinking within twenty questions.

Woman Twenty questions? And you'll let me go?

Man I'm not holding you. You can go any time you like.

She looks around, makes to take her bag, hesitates.

Woman I can't go. I'm... waiting...

Man So am I. Twenty questions. It will pass the time.

Woman All right.

Man Is it animal?

Woman Is what animal?

Man The thing you're thinking about.

Woman What thing I'm thinking about?

Man The game. Twenty questions. The game.

Woman Ah! Yes. The game.

Man Are you thinking about something?

Woman Always. And never one simple thing. A whole mad blur of things that rush one upon another, like flames in a fire. Plans and memories. Actions and regrets. Forecasts and hopes. So many things to think about.

Man Is it vegetable, then?

Woman Is this the game again? You don't want to just talk, do you?

Man Me? You're the one who hardly says a word. I'm trying hard to make the waiting bearable, while you...

Woman What are you waiting for?

Man What are *you* waiting for?

Woman I'm waiting for history to begin again. It's a funny thing. When you actually take part in history, not just live your life as an innocent bystander, but take centre stage, even in a small way, history stops. I'm waiting for it to restart.

Man You never talk about yourself. It's all ideas and... things. Like you felt nothing.

Woman You're wrong. I felt every thing. Every thing I learned, every thing I saw, every thing I knew. I felt it all. That's why I acted. In history. In time. And now history and time have stopped, as if they were cogs in a great engine turning the century and I stuck my little finger in there. So they're stopped. And I'm waiting.

Man Think of something, then. For the game.

Woman All right.

Man Is it vegetable?

Woman Yes.

Man Can you eat it?

Woman Eh… Yes… No… I'm not sure.

Man Does it grow?

Woman Yes.

Man Yes! Three questions. Three answers. It's a vegetable. It grows and maybe you can eat it. It's a flower, isn't it?

Woman No.

Man Look, you have to give the right answer if I ask the right question.

Woman I have given the right answers.

Man Maybe I'm asking the wrong questions.

Woman Maybe we're playing the wrong game.

Time passes.

Man You always say that.

Woman What?

Man Something about the game. 'It's not a game.' 'It's the wrong game.'

Woman You say it, too. And anyway, you started it.

Man I did not. You brought the bomb.

Woman The bomb didn't start it. It started years before that. Talk started it. And talk will finish it.

Man And new games, with new rules. If we can find them.

Woman Look, if you want to go on punishing yourself, you can, but...

Man But nothing. Let's get this straight. This isn't about you and me. You've done your time. And now you're free to do what you like. I'm still doing mine. But I'm learning. I'm not a victim any more. Not me. Oh no! You want to know what I am? Do you?

Woman Yes.

Man Do you really?

Woman Yes, yes.

Man I'm a survivor. I survived. Through all the pain, anguish, hurt, grief, history, time and blood. I survived. That's my legacy. Your legacy, too.

Woman You still want to punish me.

Man I don't want to punish you. What good would that do? You've served your time. She's dead. It's over. She's never coming back. I survived and this is it. No matter how long we wait, this is it.

Woman (*Looks around.*) It's not much, is it?

Man No, it's not much. Just a place and some memories and time passing into ever-shortening futures. But you survived, too. You're a survivor.

Woman I survived all right. Look, if it's all over… the whole thing… I mean, then we can say we survived *for* something.

Man Exactly.

Woman But what?

Man Life. Still, you can't build a life on a game of chance.

Woman It's not a game.

Man No. Definitely. Not a game.

Time passes.

Man It's not much of a place. Used to be a proper bus stop. With a shelter. Blown to shreds, too.

Woman I know. I remember. I was here.

Man You were here?

Woman Look, war is about targets. Collateral damage. Lists getting longer. They do this, we do that. One of ours, one of theirs. Some in uniform, some in civvies. Some legitimate, some illegitimate…

Man All dead.

Woman All dead. The lowest common denominator. The bottom line.

Man She was killed here.

Woman I know.

Man You were here.

Woman I was.

Man You've aged. I hardly recognise you.

Woman Time passes.

Time passes.

Woman We could sing. We used to do a lot of that. Inside. Keeps the spirits up.

Man I was never much of a singer. She did all the singing. Sang away. In the bath. Washing dishes. Just sitting there of an evening, on the sofa, with nothing else in the world going on, only her singing.

Sings.

And of all the sweethearts I e'er did have,
They wished I'd stay another day.

Speaks.

Sweethearts. Stay another day.

Woman "The Parting Glass". I know it. Well, bits of it. It's so hard. Remembering.

Man (*Sings.*)
Of all the money that e'er I had,
I spent it in good company.

Woman (*Sings.*)
And of all the harm I ever have done,
Alas I did to none but me.

Man
And all I've said through lack of wit,
To memory now I can't recall.

Both
Come fill to me the parting glass,
Good luck and joy be with you all.

Woman
Of all the comrades I e'er did have
They're sorry at my going away.

Man
And of all the sweethearts I e'er did have
They wished I'd stay another day.

Woman
But since it falls unto my lot
That I must go and you must not.
I'll gently rise and softly call
Good luck and joy be with you all.

Man (*Speaks.*) It's a sad song.

Woman (*Speaks.*) It's a sad time.

Man (*Looking for bus.*) Still no sign. It was a weed,
wasn't it? Not a flower. A weed.

Woman What was?

Man What you were thinking about. Twenty questions.

Woman Naw. It wasn't a weed. I was thinking about a seed. A seed. We have to move on. Ourselves, I mean.

Man It's very hard.

Woman It is. We'll always be waiting.

She takes up her suitcase and leaves.

Man Always waiting…

Sings.

If I had money enough to spend
And leisure time to sit awhile,
There is a fair maid in this town,
That sorely has my heart beguiled.
Her rosy cheeks and ruby lips
I own, she does my heart enthral.
Then fill to me the parting glass,
Good luck and joy be with you all.

He leaves.

The Shopper and the Boy

Shopper *and* **Boy** *enter, carrying a trunk. They carry it round the space a few times. They put it down facing the audience and* **Shopper** *turns her back to the audience.*

Boy No surrender!

They pick up the trunk and walk through 180 degrees so that **Shopper** *now faces the audience. They are still holding the trunk.*

Shopper Tiocfaidh ár lá!

They turn once more for **Boy** *to repeat 'No surrender!' then he faces backwards. They take the trunk back and put it down. They end with a big shoulder-shrugging sigh in unison. They open it and draw out a long length of strong blue cloth. It is as wide as the trunk. This is the river between them. They gaze at it, walk up and down its banks, gaze over it, skim stones on it, but their eyes do not meet. The take up the positions of the statues on Craigavon Bridge in Derry Londonderry, two figures with outstretched hands, not quite touching. They return to the trunk and* **Boy** *takes shaving foam, a towel and razor out of the trunk, claims centre stage, still on his side of the river.* **Shopper** *sits on her end, facing away.*

Boy (*He is preparing himself for the day. He is lathering and shaving, humming* "The Sash".) Da da dah dah dah dah daaah da dah.

He performs a little strutting walk, holding the foam and razor in front of him, draping the towel round him like a sash. He faces front and sings loudly.

It was old, but it was beautiful,
And the colours they were grand…
The sash my father wore.

Aye, my father. (*He now appears to be talking to the
mirror he is shaving in.*) I mind the first time he took me.
I mind standing at the top of Bond's Hill, looking down
at all the buses and the crowds milling around outside
the train station. Like a great army, they were. Battalions
of them in all their finery, and the river behind them
sparkling like a jewel in the August sunlight. My hands
started to sweat. My knees began to knock. (*Pause.*) Ach,
I was only a nadger. (*Looks at his palms and his knees.*)
And me da said, 'That's us, son. Remember that. Our
people. Our people.'

*He hums again, towelling off the remaining soap, turns
and steps back to the trunk as* **Shopper** *rises and comes
forward to claim centre stage, on her side of the river.*

Shopper Our people. (*Pause.*) Our people picked the
pennies out of their hair, picked the abuse out of their
ears, then picked themselves up off their knees, to gaze
bewildered and amazed at the mighty walled city. Our
people looked aghast as the march went past in a blaze of
triumphant colour.

Boy *comes forward in line with* **Shopper.**

Boy Our people marched in time and history. Our people
stepped out in tradition and power.

Shopper Our people looked on.

Shopper / **Boy** (*Facing each other.*)
Another year marked out in stamping feet.

Another year marked out in shoe leather.
Another year trodden underfoot.
Another year.

*They walk back to the trunk, stand at opposite ends and
face away from each other in The Bargaining Position.*

Shopper You first.

Boy No you.

Shopper Okay, then. (*Pause.*) I want to be able to go up
the town and shop in peace. Now you.

Boy I want to march with my brothers in our regalia on
the Twelfth of August. Now you.

Shopper (*Pause.*) Let me tell you about regalias.
Uniforms. Let me tell you about uniforms.

*She reaches into the trunk and tosses out a selection of
clothes belonging to her eleven-year-old son. She comes
to the front.* **Boy** *sits on the trunk, facing front.*

I have a wee fella going into secondary school. Michael.
Same name as his da. Quiet young fella, with kind of
mousey hair. Wonder where he got that? (*Touches her
own hair.*) He's the first. A big pile of love came out
of me and every time I look at him, I get a lump in my
throat. (*Pause.*) Anyway, he got the eleven-plus, so
he's going to the College. Black blazer. Black trousers.
Lumpy school bag.

Pause. She has picked up all the clothes.

You can't get a uniform without money. You can't get
money without work. And Michael, the da, he's not

working. No, that's not right. He is working. And so am I. Just not getting paid for it. Always working. (*Pause.*) Trying to get something to put a uniform on the boy's back.

Boy (*Still seated on the trunk.*) Aye, the uniform's the thing. The braid on the shoulders. Aye. The cap and the brassy buttons. The shoes, black and shiny as tar bubbles on a summer road.

He comes forward and **Shopper** *goes back to the trunk and sits.* **Boy** *sings / declaims.*

Oh! for the bandsman's uniform,
The braid, the button and the sash.
Oh! for the day out on the bus,
The beer, the music and the cash.
Oh! for the weltering heat of it all,
The sun like a fiery eye.
Oh! for the sound of the fife and drum
And the blaze of banners in the sky.

Shopper *moves back to the trunk and puts away the clothes.* **Boy** *moves forward and lies down, hands joined behind his head, as if he is looking at the sky.*

I mainly remember the stars, jewels for the Eleventh night, bright eyes staring down at my bare belly, rounded out with cider and beer. (*Pause.*) And the big fire, cackling and spurting. All the fellas running around mad, throwing things on the fire and running round it, trying to jump the lower reaches of its might, orange flames licking their arses. Cheers going up. (*Pauses.*) God it's great.

Turns on his arm and faces forward still lying down.

When I was a wean, ach, years ago, we used to build a hut near the bonfire, to guard it. That was the best bit. Just three or four of us, cramped into a wooden crate, so close we could smell each other's sweat. A tangy sweet smell. And Sammy Hamilton's ma sent over big jam sandwiches, door-stoppers, and our mouths got covered in red, like lipstick carelessly daubed on. (*He gets into a sitting position.*) Now I just turn up with my carry-out and feel the warm glow of it all. Seeing all the people, their faces lit up by the fire, drinking in the heat of history. All one big crowd. (*Pause.*) Together. And then the cops come.

Shopper (*Seated on trunk.*) Uniforms. Every place has them now. All the shops. It's all uniforms. Trying to make everyone look the same under cover of trying to make us look smart. (*Pause. She comes forward.*) That's one thing I like about the credit union. No uniforms. Everyone's different. They treat you like a person. Like you're someone who needs money for a uniform. (*Pause.*) They don't wear them but they gave me the money for Michael's.

Boy *stands up.*

Boy Our people got jobs with uniforms and marching and the rule of law.

Shopper Our people tried to go to college. (*Pause.*) Well, some of us anyway.

Shopper/Boy (*Chanting in unison, facing each other.*)
Another year marked out in stamping feet.
Another year marked out in shoe leather.
Another year trodden underfoot.
Another year.

*They return to the ends of the trunk, facing away from
each other. The Bargaining Position.*

Shopper You first this time.

Boy Okay. (*Pause.*) I want your people to stop calling it
'the College' as if there was only one. (*Pause.*) I want to
be able to get a job. The army's all right, but I want to be
able stay in my own town. And call it what we want to
call it. Londonderry.

Shopper I want a job, too. But not for peanuts. And not
in a uniform. You put on a uniform and they think they
can push you around.

Shopper *takes out a baby carrier, a baby and a credit
union book.* **Boy** *lifts a carry-out bag, blue plastic with
full cans in it, from the trunk.* **Shopper** *sits down, facing
forward.* **Boy** *lurches forward. He is slightly drunk.*

Boy (*As to friends.*) I'll talk to them. Leave it to me. It's
all right. (*He comes forward to talk to the cops.*) Yes.
What about yeez? Someone has to work on the Eleventh
night, I suppose? Do you want a can? (*He proffers the
bag jokingly.*) Only kidding, officer.

Shopper (*Comes forward, talking to a credit union
clerk.*) Aye, she's the youngest. No more after her.
(*Laughs.*) Aye, I know what you mean. If it's not one
thing it's another. At least that's the uniform for the eldest
sorted out. Aye, give me cash.

Boy (*Talking to policeman, glances back over his
shoulder.*) Ach, no. It'll be grand. No way is it going
to reach those wires. Complaints? Yeez have had
complaints! Noise. Ach, yeez can see for yourselves. It's

all under control. A bit of a laugh, that's all. Anyway, we always have one round here, every year. Yeez know that. Hail, rain or shine. Yeez did it yourselves. It's a tradition and I don't need to tell you, officer, how important that is. The ties that bind and all that. Gives us something to be proud of. Stick out our chests. And our bellies. (*Sticks them both out, laughs, then muses.*) We're drawn to the fire like beautiful moths, warmed in the pride of doing something we have always done.

Shopper I know what you mean. But what use is pride to people like us? You can't boil it, grill it, fry it, steam it or bake it. Weans don't grow fat on it. (*Pause.*) Fivers would be great.

Boy Look, what do you want us to do? Put out the fire and huddle in the darkness? Hide ourselves in the shadows where no one could see us? Go into the wilderness and wander like a lost tribe? No way. We have more pride than that. You mightn't be able to eat pride, but it can fill you up. And everyone needs something to be proud about. You're proud of the law, aren't you?

Shopper You're right. There's one law for the rich and another law for the poor. But that'll not bother the likes of me too much. Anyway, whoever makes the law rules the roost.

Boy Exactly. But do they know what it's like to be out on the Eleventh night and to feel that this is the Big One. That all you've ever wanted was to keep this night going, this night and every night stretching on into the future, with everything staying the same and everybody knowing where they stand and everything worked out.

Shopper Naw, we can't go back to that again. Things'll have to change. (*Pause*.) Anyway, I have the money now and I'll be able to get the uniform. Better get it today. Money is like water. It'll run through your fingers before you know where you are. (*Pause.*) Ach, you're right. They're marching today. The town will be blocked off.

Boy Look, a few of us could block off the top end there and make sure no more stuff is put on it. We'll keep the wee lads away from it and make sure the noise is kept down. (*Pause.*) You want it put out? You're calling the fire brigade? Do you want a riot?

Shopper Riot Corner. I always knew it as that. William Street and Rossville Street. A battleground.

They stand facing forwards.

Boy Erne Gardens.

Shopper Quarry Street.

They continue in this way, reciting a litany of street names from different parts of the city.

Roulston Avenue	Lisfannon Park
Lapwing Way	Elmwood Road
Seymour Gardens	Moyola Drive
Wapping Lane	Cable Street

Shopper / **Boy** (*Chanting in unison, facing each other.*)
Another year marked out in stamping feet.
Another year marked out in shoe leather.
Another year trodden underfoot.
Another year.

They return to the trunk, put props away and take up The Bargaining Position.

Shopper I want to be able to walk the streets in safety whenever I want, wherever I want.

Boy I want to be able to live anywhere in this town if I want to.

Shopper I don't want anyone telling me I drove them away.

Boy And I want to be able to go into the city centre and be myself.

Shopper I want to be able to call the city what I want to call it. Derry.

They return to the trunk and they take out Laurel and Hardy masks. He puts on a cowboy hat and comes forward.

Boy (*Sings joyously, line dancing.*)
Oh! for the blaze of coloured lights
That dance in the river that night.
Oh! for the crowds all gathered round
Dressed up to make a sight.
Oh! for the bangers, the beer and the laughs
The costumes, the colour and the craic.
Oh! for the Hallowed eve that falls
Across the city so black.

Dashing about, gazing upwards.

There's a big one. Listen to that. Just above the clock of the Guildhall. Whooo! That's class. Did you hear it? You see them before you hear the bang, like the two weren't connected. Like the bang came from the hulking hills behind there. That's where my da said his family came from. (*Points.*) Catherine Wheels. In mid-air. How do they do that? Ooooh! A big starburst, going off like a radiant bomb, sending shards of itself into the sky so I can see the faces of everyone around me, hanging onto these railings, at this roundabout, looking over the river to the centre of the city.

Steps forward and takes off his hat and speaks directly to the audience.

Why? Well, you get a better view for one thing. You might think there would be more craic over there in the Guildhall Square with the bands and the crowds, but you get a better view from across here. You're up a wee bit so the fireworks don't seem to press over you so much. It doesn't mean that I'm letting the city to them over there. Just because they're filling up the Square and listening to the bands. We like dressing up as much as anybody. It's just that what you see depends on how you look at it. And where you look at it from. So that the same thing can be different. Like the river itself. (*Looks down at blue sheet.*) Different, depending on what bank you live on.

Puts the hat back on again, points upwards.

Brilliant! Fantastic! I hope there's another one of those starbursts.

He makes his way back to the trunk, sits and looks away, hat off. **Shopper** *comes forward with the mask in her hand.*

Shopper Tearing up sheets to make a ghost. Ripping up a black dress of my mother's to make a witch's cloak. He had to get wee rushes and twigs to make a broom. Ach, it's for the weans really.

Points upwards excitedly.

Oh! Look at that. They're like dangling jewels, beacons gliding in the black sea of night. Ah! that's lovely. Fire bursting. Fire works a miracle. I love it. You can put on things. Layers. You can be yourself, but amplified like music coming out of great speakers. You can be on a stage. You can be an actress. You can be someone. A ghost. OOOOOOOO! A devil. Come burn with me! A vampire. Let me drink your blood! (*Puts on mask.*) Laurel…

Boy (*Puts on mask and calls out.*) … and Hardy.

He gets up and comes forward.

Shopper / **Boy** (*Chant, once each, then once together.*) Another fine mess you've got me into!

Shopper / **Boy** (*Facing each other.*)
Another year marked out in stamping feet.
Another year marked out in shoe leather.
Another year trodden underfoot.
Another year.

They return to the trunk, put away their masks and take up The Bargaining Position.

Shopper I want something more than bread and circuses. I want something more than a spectacle. (*Pause.*) I want esteem.

Boy I want celebrations, with flags and emblems, bands and marching feet.

Shopper I want to see the tricolour flying in the wind. High up.

Boy I want to have children and know they'll be proud to be British.

Shopper I want my children to know who they are and where they come from.

Shopper *lifts a listening device from trunk and pins it to her shirt. She flicks the pause button on the tape player inside the trunk and we hear baby sleeping sounds. Breathing and snuffling. She puts a green tea towel over her shoulder and comes forward, arms crossed.* **Boy** *sits on the trunk.*

Shopper She's bad with asthma. That's why we got this thing. The other part of it sits on the top of her cot and I go round the house with her breathing in my ear. (*Pause.*) Washing up, drying up, cooking. And listening to her breathing. Like a death rattle put on hold.

Clasps her neck with both hands and prays.

Please don't let her die. Let it be a cot, not a coffin. Let her grow up strong and tall to run around with other wee girls. Swap friendship bracelets, braided coloured strings on her tiny wrist. Skip rope. (*Pause.*) I did it myself.

She smiles in remembering and she twirls the tea towel as in skipping and chants the rhyme.

Teddy Bear, Teddy Bear, burl right round.
Teddy Bear, Teddy Bear, touch the ground.
Teddy Bear, Teddy Bear, show off your shoes.
Teddy Bear, Teddy Bear, that will do.
Teddy Bear, Teddy Bear, run up stairs.
Teddy Bear, Teddy Bear, say your prayers.
Teddy Bear, Teddy Bear, switch off the light.
Teddy Bear, Teddy Bear, spell goodnight.
G-O-O-D-N-I-G-H-T.

Swinging on poles, skipping on ropes and 'Play the ball against the wall'. Someone taught me all that. I don't know. Maybe it was just in the blood, like we were born into it.

She looks back to the trunk.

I want to tell her so many things, so many things she should know about who she is and who we are. I want her to have more chances than me. Michael's all right, but we were too young. Anyway, there must be more to life than bringing up kids with a man on the dole. (*Pause.*) I want to teach her to dance, but she's a bit young yet. I was a champion myself, you know. Yes. Ach, all right, then.

Dances some Irish dance steps.

I've started singing her songs. Songs my mother taught me. Just sounds really, because I'm not sure what the words mean. Something strange happened to our language. It became more beautiful the more we lost it. Maybe she'll learn it properly. I hope so. (*Pause as baby sounds become crying.*) Ach, wait. Wait a wee minute now. Wait a wee minute.

She goes back to the trunk, takes the baby out, wrapped in a blanket. **Boy** *takes out a bowler hat and an umbrella and stands on the trunk facing backwards. She sits on the edge of the trunk and sings a lullaby.*

Fill, fill a rún ó,
Fill, a rún ó, is ná himigh uaim.
Fill orm, a chuisle's a stór,
Agus chifidh tú an glóir má fhilleann tú.

Boy *comes forward and* **Shopper** *drops her voice, but continues to croon the lullaby.*

Boy There were no lullabies in the trenches. No sleeping, with the scurrying of the rats, the dankness of the water, the smell of death and gas everywhere. How could you sleep with that? When we marched in answer to our country's call, did we know our sacrifice would be a bloodbath?

I am the last Old Contemptible.
For the first time ever I was alone at the cenotaph
And the "Last Post" was played for me.
The drizzle and the drone of the trumpets hemmed me in.
I looked at the wreath and stepped back, putting one foot
Firmly in the grave.
I'll be dead by Christmas.

I have a son in Canada.
His children sound like television to me.
My daughter, in England, she'll come home to bury me
and cry.
And return to England, leaving no one to tend my grave.

But I will make no surrender to the bleak bliss of death.
I will rage quietly to the end though that end will be a
blessed relief.
A relief from the shells and the groans.
And my friends calling to me.
I hear them.
Tommy Watson, Vernon Lumley, Cecil Harding.
I am coming soon.

Tommy Watson – he always had to be smoking
something.
Always had a smoke of something.
And he shared it.
We shared everything.
Food. Shelter. Fear.
The stench of fear makes me tremble even now.

Tinnitus, the doctor said.
Twerp.
The noises in my ears were old age, he said.
The fool didn't know they had the freshness of youth,
The rawness of boys out on a spree
And the bitterness of young men dying
Like flies swatted lazily in the summer.

The noises got worse after Tillie died.
Then Thiepval roared in my head
And the slime of the Somme slurped around.
But I marched on,
Each year at the Cenotaph as my last comrades faded
around me
Until now I am finally alone.

I march on even now, always marching
Ceaselessly slogging forwards and downwards.
Down to death and waste.
I came to manhood in waste.
Tommy Watson scythed by shrapnel, Vernon Lumley
gassed,
Cecil Harding on a barbed-wire spit.
My God left me that day and never returned.
The horrors drove him out and the shame kept him away.

Will they be there? Will they have marched on yet
further?

No! They'll be there.
Tommy, Vernon and Cecil.
And Tommy will have a smoke of something like always.

I will make no final surrender.
I will make a reunion and I will go forward to my
comrades,
Ever forward to my comrades.

And Tillie.
And the quiet! Oh, the sweet quiet!

Shopper's *voice comes back up and she sings the lullaby
again.* **Boy** *returns to the trunk and puts the bowler and
the umbrella inside. She puts the baby and the listening
device away also and they come forward and face each
other.*

Shopper / **Boy** (*Chanting in unison.*)
Another year marked out in stamping feet.
Another year marked out in shoe leather.
Another year trodden underfoot.
Another year.

*They face forward and click their fingers to begin a
synchronised dance routine as they chant / rap.*

It's the Big One.
It's come at last.
The one we've waited for.

It's the Big One.
The relief of Derry.
The boom goes up today.

It's the Big One.
Get my uniform.
Step out onto the street.

It's the Big One.
August Twelfth.
Gather up the bands.

*They return to the trunk and take up The Bargaining
Position.*

Boy I want to celebrate my civil and religious liberties.

Shopper I want respect. Not mere tolerance. Respect.

Boy I want to march my traditional route.

Shopper I want to do what I have to do and I don't want to be abused doing it.

Boy *takes a trowel and a brick out of the trunk and comes forward.* **Shopper** *sits on trunk.*

Boy I'm an Apprentice Boy. (*Pause.*) I'm a boy apprentice. Or at least I was. You see, I was just out of my time when they let me go. Thirteen of us. The Brave Thirteen. Brickies. Chippies. Sparks. All the houses were nearly built anyway. No more work for us, they said. It had nothing to do with the fact that they'd have to pay us men's wages. Nothing to do with that at all.

He goes down on one knee, scoops mortar and generally works as if laying bricks.

I love the heft of a brick in my hand, the weighty lump of it. And the way a wall would build itself in front of your eyes, all regular and solid so you could look up at it and be amazed. Feel protected. Secure in its mortared embrace. Neat, eh? Like the clip of a trowel. Spare and regular.

He softly sings a snatch of "Derry's Walls" *as he lays the brick, continues humming the tune as* **Shopper** *speaks from standing on the trunk.*

Shopper Walls of police and soldiers. Walls of bricks and mortar. Walls to keep you in. Walls to keep you out. Walls to look up at. Walls to look down from. Walls to go through the gates of. Walls to walk along in the sun. Walls for marches. Walls for protests. Walls for graffiti. Walls for murals. Walls for us. Walls for them. Walls for everyone.

Boy I remember all apprentices. The ones who shut the gates. The ones who built the ships, the factories and the bridges of this great country.

He puts the brick in the centre of the river, fixing it with the trowel.

It's the big day. Time to get the uniform on.

He returns to the trunk. She gets down and takes out the chest carrier and the baby. He takes out an Apprentice Boy's sash. They put them on and come forward.

Shopper (*Talking to a soldier.*) Look, I tried to explain to you, Corporal Clod. Ferguson's on William Street doesn't have his size.

Boy Yes, Vernon. How's it going?

Shopper I have the money today and I want to buy it today. It's not a big thing. I don't need the whole town blocked off just so's I can buy a uniform for the boy.

Boy Yes, Tommy. What about ye? Any fags on ye, son?

Shopper You've a grand uniform on you. Does it make you feel bigger? More of a man?

Boy Cecil. Haven't seen ye in years. Great day for it, eh?

Shopper Look, why don't you go back to your wife and weans over in Birmingham, or wherever it is you're from, and not be bothering me. I have to get up to Carlisle Road. To Moore's. They'll have the uniform.

Boy Andrew. John. Wilson. Ian. 'Bout ye, big fella? Form up there, lads.

Shopper Look, I'll just go up around the walls, then? They're all blocked off, too. Right, then. The Diamond it is.

Boy Right, then. Move off.

She begins to move round town. He crosses the river, marching and waving. They are choreographed to pass each other and not meet. The noise of his marching feet increases to a crescendo as she waits to cross the street through the march.

Shopper There's Moore's. Can I cross now? Is there a gap? I'm going now.

She dashes forward, he marches on and they collide. Freeze and hold. Then they return to the trunk. They take off props and de-role, coming forward.

Woman We know this is no way to end a play. But we've gone as far as we can go.

Man We've said all the things that we can say. We've shown you all the things we know.

Woman It's more than about shopping.

Man It's more than about marching.

Woman Can people change? Can the world be changed?

Man How could a better ending be arranged? (*Pause.*)
Will we leave it to them?

*They both look at the audience, then back at each other,
then face forward, smiling.*

Both (*Confidently.*) Yes.

Without the Walls

There are city walls. **Chorus** *appears from behind the walls, two men and one woman. They are wearing lengths of coloured cloth – red, green, orange – draped over their black costumes, signifying they are elders / leaders.*

Chorus
Without the walls, there is no city.
Without the walls, none of us could live here.
Without the walls, there is a body.

Within there is order and law
But also disorder and dissent.
There has been a war.
A bloody conflict of divided loyalties
That has left the city beaten, transfixed.
Now is a time of change,
Some even speak of healing
For the pouring on of balm
And the licking of wounds.
It is a delicate time, fragile as spring shoots,
Delicate as gossamer.

We face so many problems
And we hardly face each other
Where lately our sons and daughters fought each other.
Over barricades, in bombings,
Late-night shootings, the raiding of houses,
The shoot to kill,
The shoot to maim.

We have seen so many bodies
And bits of bodies. That one more
Without the walls is no surprise.

But who will claim it?
The city? The family?

Chorus *returns behind the walls.* **Woman** *and* **Senator**
come out from opposite sides.

Scene 1

Woman Thank you for agreeing to see me.

Senator I am your Senator. I am here for every citizen.

Woman You know it is my brother who lies without the
walls, swathed in a plastic bin liner. His life, and his death,
wasted. Three days he has lain there, white tape cordoning
him off so that only the magpies can circle him in the
ditch. We want to bring him home.

Senator We can arrange it. Go home and the police will
arrange it.

Woman I am here to ask you not to do that.

Senator But it is the way. Why should your brother be
different?

Woman Because the times are different. Our river has
run red, but now begins to clear. Old people put food on
the window ledges and in their yards to entice the doves
to return and stay. Young people take to the streets in
carnivals. The guns are silent and the elders are talking. It
is a time of facing up to histories. Problems. Futures.

Senator Even so, it is a policing matter. Leave it to
them. No one must remove the body or perform the rites.
If you disobey this edict, I promise you…

Woman I had two brothers, now both dead. You knew one. He was in your guard. He fell protecting the city.

Senator He was loyal, yes.

Woman So was the other. Loyal.

Senator But not to the city.

Woman He would say he was, were he able to speak. But he is without words, his mouth stuffed with plastic, a hole in the back of his head, and I must speak for him. I won't cry and I won't beg, though it would be natural. And what you're doing defies all natural law. The brother who was in your guard was given a funeral by the city. My other brother deserves no less.

Senator The honours for the dead are not the same for the wicked and the just.

Woman Who are the just you speak of? How can anyone know, when two brothers chose different sides? Your position, the fount of justice, stands high and dry before us.

Senator
Leave us. Go. Do not anger us further.
And remember my edict, loud and clear.
If your brother's body you go near.
The city will strike you, without fear.
And make you pay a price that's dear.

Woman *exits.*

Senator
Without the walls, there is a body.
Without the law, there is no order.

Without the police, there is no authority.
Guard!

Exit **Senator**.

Scene 2

Enter **Guard** *from opposite side, masked and carrying a
truncheon.*

Guard
I am the helper, I help.
I am the hero, I save.
I am arbiter, I resolve.
I am the defender, I protect.
I am the avenger, I punish.
I am the servant.
I do the bidding of the powerful.

Aye, a policeman's lot is not a happy one
And so the song would have it.
And I can tell you it is so
Without a jot or caveat.
For who would stand before the mob
That flings abuse and thole it.
For who would watch a colleague shot
– a life lost – and chase those who stole it?
And who would come when you call at night
Because your neighbour's ranting?
Who would help you catch the thief
Who trespasses on your landing?

Aye, indeed the policeman's lot is not a happy one.
Indeed the song would have it.
I've stood knee-deep in colleagues' blood

And wondered was it worth it?
But the smell of sweat together made
In Land Rovers grey and sullen,
Gives hope we'll come out alive
Despite culvert bomb and bullet.

And who will mourn for us that gave our lives
For your security and safety?
Who will say that we were wrong
To sing and dance the politicians' song?

Between a rock and a hard place, we
Between the state and the community.
He watches over his shoulder,
Never daring to be bolder.
Always seeking a ready vote
While crime and violence grabs us by the throat.

You huddle in your houses, you
And expect us to solve your problems, too.
Your daughter raped, your son battered,
You call us out as if it mattered
What religion, culture, identity we hold.
Of course it's complex. We've been told
To sensitise and harmonise and realise
That our city, it's no surprise,
Is not a unitary monolith
Though all the citizens draw same breath.

Aye, indeed a policeman's lot is not a happy one.
And now this matter's come to light
And what are we to do?
The politicians' bidding? Surely that is right.
I'm just the same as you or you.
I can only do what I'm allowed to do.

Senator (*Off stage.*) Guard!

Guard *shrugs and exits.*

Enter **Chorus**, *each carrying a chair.*

Chorus
The times are changing.
Even the seasons are awry.
Spring is blowy, stormy, cold.
September roasts us.
And January is so mild the birds nest too early.

And we, elders of the city,
Sit down to face our differences
And each other.

Member 1 (*Orange scarf.*)
Ours is the badge of loyalty.
We hold to the city and right and law.
Ours is the mark of sacrifice
Defence and preservation.
Surrender was never a word we used.
And yet now in changed times,
Who knows?

Member 2 (*Green scarf.*)
Ours is the badge of rebellion.
We hold to history, rights and justice.
Ours is the mark of struggle,
Insurrection and change.
Defeat was never a word we used.
And yet now in changed times,
Who knows?

Member 3 (*Red scarf.*)
It's all up for grabs now.
We meet in forums and seminars.
Megaphone diplomacy, proximity talks,
Positions, soundings, understandings.
Our river has run red with blood.
We have fought each other.
Our streets defiled, our walls breached.
Our very hearts seared by the freezing fire of death.
And we are expected to move on?

This is but one city in an ageing Empire.
Across the water the Imperial Seat
Has power to oversee our deliberations.

So, our cultures clash and they have the final say.
Our police collapse and they have the final say.
Our jobless rise and they have the final say.
Our children wallow in poverty and they have the final say.
Do we have any say at all?

Exit **Chorus***, carrying chairs.*

Scene 3

Enter **Guard***, can of beer in hand.*

Guard
In this city, drink's a curse.
Have no pity, drugs are worse.
I'm just thankful I can sup
By the tankful from life's cup.

Enter **Senator***, angry.* **Guard** *comes to attention and salutes.*

Senator Come to attention, take your heed.

Guard I do your bidding though my feet bleed.

Senator You saw the woman here today.

Guard That I did to my dismay.

Senator She carried stories of our lapse.

Guard She carried the paper and a bag of baps.

Senator Her plea must not be accepted.

Guard That is just what I expected.

Senator Here is my edict, loud and clear.

Guard Open ears that yeez might hear.

Senator No one will perform the rites.

Guard The body rests there overnight.

Senator It is a policing matter.

Guard I'll be early on the batter.

Senator Do our bidding, uphold the law.

Guard I'll go, then tell you what I saw.

Exit **Guard**.

Senator
It is a trick.
It's a dodgy one this.

Because the times are dodgy.
Everything is up for grabs.
Even my job. Even the law.
Sometimes I long for simpler days
When everyone knew their place
And there was obedience and law.

The woman questions me
And the law's authority.

I long for happier times.
When everything was clearer.
When you could say,
'Our city' and know what you meant.
'Our politics, our government, our police.'

The rebels want a piece of the action.
And I'm fair-minded, let's agree.

The elders meet in new convention.
I hope they give this due attention.

Exit **Senator**.

Scene 4

Enter **Woman.**

Woman (*Sings.*)
I had two brothers, one fair, one dark.
They ran like lambs, they sang like larks.
I had two brothers, so tall, so strong.
One chose 'right', the other chose 'wrong'.

I had two brothers now dead, now dead.
One lies in the ground, a stone at his head.

The other brother, I go to now.
And by his side my head I'll bow.

It was no wrong that took him there,
Without the walls of this city fair.
It was cause of justice and of rights denied,
That made him take the other side.

I had two brothers, I mourn them both.
My tears fall from me as I go forth,
To do what nature has just decreed,
And the city's edict I will not heed.

Speaks.

I will crawl like a sneak thief
Under cover of the night
And anoint my second brother.
They are sullen with me, his former comrades –
My first brother was in the city guard –
They say I am not to be trusted.
And who do I trust at this time?
The Guard who raided and defiled our house?

Were it mere force we needed
Any brute would do the mannish thing.
But if our voices are not heeded
In the calls we make and the songs we sing
Then it will never change
And the brutes will have their way.

It's a nostalgia thing.
Of something I saw on telly.
But is there a bobby somewhere,
A Dixon of Dock Green,
A lime-eyed denizen of Garda Patrol,

Whose steely smile and broad shoulders
Stood between us and hell,
Sheltered and succoured all?

I go to do the right thing.
If the law is anything it will aid me.
I am no damsel in distress.
I am a hero, only by necessity.
People like me just want a quiet life.
But when you see something, you must act.

I defy unnatural laws and edicts.
He was my brother.
And law and police above all else
Have a duty to guard the rights and liberties
Of each and every citizen.
I know what I am doing is wrong.
Disloyal to the city.
But I am loyal to my family.

Exit **Woman**.

Scene 5

Enter **Senator**. **Journalists** *are seated in the audience, unmasked.*

Senator
Calm down, calm down, we don't want a riot.
Can everybody please be quiet.
Now let us begin this Press Conference
And I hope you won't take too much offence
If I answer questions one by one.
That's it now. Let's have one from you, son.

Journalist 1
Reports come in thick and fast
And here's one I hold, the last,
Which says a body lies without the walls
And you, Senator, have refused all calls
To have it removed for burial.
Do you issue a denial?

Senator
I deny all denials.
I fillet all files.
I cover all controversy.
I bury all baloney.
I refuse all righteousness.
I wash my hands of this sad mess.
Next question.

Journalist 2
Is it true a woman has buried the body, her brother,
In open defiance of your clear order?

Senator
What is said may well be true
And if so, well, she will rue.
To enter the city you must use a gate
And she that has defied the State
Will find all barred to her, and further
Will she be bound and gagged as if for murder.
Her disobedience it is clear to see
Is an offence to all civility.
The law is there to be obeyed
And Rulers' rule cannot be swayed
By snivelling claims or calls to arms
Or media hype and political charms.

Exit **Senator.** *Exit* **Journalists**.

Enter **Chorus.**

Chorus
Police for crime and theft.
Police for fraud and usury.
Police for bombs and shootings.
Police for state security.

Police for rape and sex abuse.
Police for brutal murder.
Police for festivals and shows.
Police for onc another.

Police for on-street drinking.
Police for youthful mayhem.
Police for protests and marches.
Police for us and police for them.
Police for everyone.

Exit **Chorus.**

Scene 6

Enter **Senator.** *Enter* **Guard** *and* **Woman**, *manacled.*

Senator You have defied my edict. You have defied the
city.

Woman It is no city if it takes orders from one voice.

Senator The city is king.

Woman
Yes, if the city is a desert.
As you know, Great Senator,

There is no consensus
About the city and its affairs.
Ours is a divided place.

Senator
You would have it, then, that we succumb
To the potent bullet and the deadly bomb?
Your brother's comrades, friends in arms,
Be sent to fetch him and say the charms,
That they perform the final rites
Who lately…

Woman
I would have it that without all arms pointing in the same
direction
No one is safe.
Power comes from the barrel of a gun, yes.
But it is people who pull the triggers.
How do we make the city safe for everyone to walk in?
How do we turn away from all your 'security' talking?
You surround yourself with history, culture, singularity.
How can all citizens be loyal to this city?

Senator
They can begin by obeying the law.
They can begin by supporting the police.
They can begin by ceasing insurrection.
They can begin by being citizens.
Take her away.

Guard
Here my duty, here today
Guarding Beauty, come what may.
Tearful sister, in grief and rage,
As I commit her to a cage.

Exit **Guard** *and* **Woman**. *Exit* **Senator**.

Enter **Chorus.**

Chorus
Here Roe runs over the red stones,
And the wind sighs in the Mournes.
Here Sperrin heather shivers,
Lagan, Bann and Foyle rivers
Course in tumult to the sea
Without regard for you or me.

Here heroes such as Sorley Boy,
Mary Ann McCracken and her brother Henry Joy,
Cú Chulainn fierce and Colm Cille mild
Fought and laughed, slept and smiled
And then fell down to become the clay
We dig and plough and walk each day.

Earth has no wonders greater than us
And yet, being earthly, why all the fuss?
We fight and bicker, shout and squawk,
But find it hard to simply talk.
And harder still to simply listen.
Do we know what we are missing?

Exit **Chorus**.

Scene 7

Enter **Guard.**

Guard
What do you want me to do?
I have colluded with certain others
Including the woman's other brother.

Loyal was he, and within the walls,
Ardent in response to calls
For defence and service to security.
Why shouldn't he work with me?
I hear some say I gave him files
Who's to say – there were so many –
If I actually gave him any?

It doesn't look good, she is hung.
What more could I have done?
It was a simple policing matter.
Ha! Just listen to my chatter.
Simple… it's never that.
Sort this out with a baseball bat!

Enter **Senator**.

Senator Speak, say what is to be said.

Guard The woman was caged and now is dead.

Senator She did this for lack of hope.

Guard She did it with a length of rope.

Senator Cries go up, the very air is tragic.

Guard I saw it plain. There is no magic.

Senator It's a weighty thing, the right to rule.

Guard For democrats who play the fool.

Senator How do we solve this new omission?

Guard Will there be a truth commission?

Exit **Guard**.

Scene 8

Senator
Without the walls, there is a body.
Within there is a woman hanged.

I am defeated. I am alone.
I am broken. Bare boned.
I am lost. All power gone.

Let the night come dark and cold.
Let the bleakest winter come and fold
The city in its maw
That we might learn to change the law.

Change: it is a mighty word.
Hard to swallow, tastes like curd.
Yet without change, all is lost.
And we will pay – and pay – the cost.

Only death is truly democratic.
No other act so automatic.
We make things, hone them from our hands.
The city serves its own demands.

So we must make a law that serves.
A law that all citizens deserve.
And arguments must take account
Of every voice, within, without.

This city is a divided place.
And law and policing must the future face.
Can we create the rule of safety
From the changing needs of our security?

Exit **Senator**.

Enter **Chorus**.

Chorus
Without the walls, there is no city.
Without the walls, none of us could live here.
Without the walls, there is a body.

Within there is order and law
But also disorder and dissent.
Within, there is a woman hanged.

It was a simple policing matter.
There is no such thing.

Disband, reform, decrease, revise, retrain,
And after that what policing will remain?
Help us face these problems.

What can we say, for you?
What do you want us to do?

Exit **Chorus.**

It's Only a Brick

Man *and* **Woman** *watching TV.*

Woman Hey! I know the answer to that. So do you. We were talking about it last week. We could have millions.

We hear smashing glass. A brick is thrown in.

Man What the f—!

Woman Oh my God! (*Beat.*) Don't touch it!

Man It's only a brick.

Woman Only!

Man Well, it could have been…

Woman Don't even say it!

Man If I get the bastards who…

Woman Who done it?

Man Who do you think?

Woman But how can they know about us?

Man Everybody knows about us. It's a small country.

Woman Aye.

Man You okay?

Woman Aye. (*Beat*.) Should we go out and look?

Man Not yet. Wait a bit.

Woman Did you hear a car?

Man No. Did you?

Woman I'm not sure.

Man Probably just ran off. Bloody cowards.

Woman Someone will have seen something. Some of the neighbours must have…

Man Nobody saw nothing. Even if they did, they'd say nothing.

Woman Will we phone…

Man Are you crazy?

Woman Best do nothing.

Man Keep the head down.

Woman It's only a brick, right?

Man Yeh. It's only a brick.

The dead abound, the dead abound.
How do we keep them in the ground?

Production Details 2

The legacy of the past is a crucial element in the future we build for ourselves. The vexed question of facing this legacy generally is dramatised in the play *AH 6905*. The specific case of Bloody Sunday is in the play *Scenes from an Inquiry*. The sketch *The Saville Inquiry London Scenarios* delivered a simulation for families of the dead in advance of moving to London for sessions of the Saville Inquiry into the events of Bloody Sunday.

AH 6905 was first produced by Sole Purpose Productions at The Playhouse, Derry Londonderry, on 13 October 2005. The director was Dave Duggan, the producer was Jonathan Burgess and the actor was Darren Greer. A man, inside whose body all the horrors of the conflict are lodged, waits in hospital for an operation to have the truth cut out of him. An adaptation and production of this play took place in Kabul, Afghanistan, in 2008.

Scenes from an Inquiry was first produced by Sole Purpose Productions at The Playhouse, Derry Londonderry, on 31 January 2002. The director was Dave Duggan, the shadow film was by Jan Vaclav Caspers and the company was Jackie Duddy, Caoimhe Farren and Sarah Wray. It poeticises the Inquiry, imagining and elevating the language of the testimonies and the questioning so that something of the greater human experience might be made public. RTÉ broadcast my radio adaptation in 2003.

The Saville Inquiry London Scenarios were first produced under commission from Cúnamh and the Bloody Sunday Families by Sole Purpose Productions at the Mount Errigal Hotel, Letterkenny, County Donegal, on 12 October 2002, as a simulation experience for family members before attending hearings in London. The director was Dave Duggan. Set construction was by Jim Keys and the company was Patricia Byrne, Jonathan Burgess, Jim Keys, Caoimhe Farren, Tony Doherty and Stuart Chapman.

AH 6905

Danny *is in pyjamas, slippers and dressing gown. He is
dozing in one of a scatter of three chairs in a room at the
end of a hospital ward. He comes to after a few moments.
It is visiting time.*

Scene 1

What kept you? (*Beat.*) Didn't fancy visiting the Lion's
den? You've finally come to see Daniel in the Lion's den.
(*Yawn.*)

Right. I was just... I didn't think there'd be so many.
(*Beat.*) I didn't think there'd be so few. I... (*Yawn.*)

Naw, we won't go back to the ward. I'm the only one
here. Sit where you are. We're fine here. (*Beat.*)

You can smoke, but don't you bother. (*Beat.*) Well, here
we are. You. Me. The Lion. Arrrgh. (*Roars and laughs.*)

I suppose you want the latest bulletin. Well, it's tomorrow.
Yeh. Tomorrow! How many are there? I haven't a clue.
All of them I suppose. The full Panel. They said – Daniel,
it's got to come out. You've had it for the past thirty-odd
years. We've got to cut it out.

Truth recovery they call it.

Ach, I know. I'm riddled with it. The past. The truth.
The truth of the past. All through me. Stuff that
happened between 1969 – remember that? – when the
country collapsed into crisis under its own weight – and

2005 – with the stuttering Peace Process continuing. All that stuff is lodged between my ribs, behind my liver and across my kidneys. Whole episodes of slaughter, mayhem and callousness are scattered among my vital organs. Shootings, bombings, maiming – all through me. Over thirty years of it.

Then there's the complications. The things themselves were bad enough, but the complications are harder to deal with. The cover-ups, the denials, the disappeared, the lost files, the negligence. Dosed with complications I am.

Everyone has a right to life, liberty. And security. If I thought everything was sorted and secure, I'd be a lot happier about this truth recovery. It's because everything is still so up in the air that I'm struggling with it.

Daniel, they said, we need to give you a number. AH 6905. A number? You're not making a statistic out of me, I said. I didn't come in here to have the truth cut out of me and stuck in a file. Don't worry, Daniel, they said. It's a truth recovery process. It's for your own good. You're 1969 to 2005. That'll cover it. We'll cut it all out of you, Daniel.

Chants.

Oh! Danny boy, the pipes, the pipes are calling. (*Laughs.*)

Pause.

Well, I told them to forget it. I'm not going through with it I said. I'm out of here asap. You can't force me. I told them. I'm telling you. You can't make me.

He looks up as if he hears voices around him.

No. Stop calling me. Don't. Don't. Please no, not now.

The dead abound, the dead abound.
How do we keep them in the ground?
The past remains, the past remains.
How do we satisfy its claims?
The truth cries out, the truth cries out.
How do we still that urgent shout?

What do you want?

A spasm of pain hits him.

Twinkle, twinkle, little car,
How I wonder where you are?
Blasted high into the sky,
There I go now, see me fly.
Twinkle, twinkle, little car,
How I wonder where you are?
Now I ponder who did this?
Killed me with their bomber's kiss.
Broke me so they might be free,
Did they ask this price of me?
Tell me, please, that I may know,
Then to heaven I will go.
Twinkle, twinkle, little car,
How I wonder where you are?

I'm okay. I'll be grand. They just possess me every now
and then.

(*Sings.*) Bewitched, bothered and bewildered, am I.
(*Slight laugh.*)

Scene 2

The more I think about it, the more I realise that the big
question is, 'Why did it happen?' (*Thinks, beat.*) People
do bad things to other people. All sorts of reasons.
Defence. Fear. Hate. In the name of loyalty. In the name
of law and order. In the name of politics. Desire. Change.
Will I ever know why it is that people did those things?
Except that… people do bad things to other people.

I know that's not enough. I know it's not.

No, I did not have a good night's sleep. I can't sleep at
night. Because of the affront. (*Beat.*) Yes, the affront.
That's right, the affront. I have the right to know the
truth. Who's going to keep it from me? Ach, now, Daniel,
it wouldn't be good for you. Let us be the judge of how
much truth you could take. No one could survive that
much truth. Not even you, Danny boy.

From glen to glen, eh? Great hordes of the dead and
injured marching from glen to glen and down the
mountainside, blood dripping from them, their wounds
gaping wide, great mouths screaming the wrong done
to them. Yes, I hear you. Look, there they come, massed
tighter than trees in a dense wood, mouth wounds
wrenched open, begging me to find the who and the why.

He looks up as if he hears voices around him.

Leave me be! Leave me be! I can never get the truth for
you. What use is the truth to the dead?

The dead abound, the dead abound.
How do we keep them in the ground?

What do you want to know?

A spasm of pain hits him.

When the crisis became occupation
Resistance rose to be an option.
It became a matter of defence.
How could I sit upon the fence?
So I swore allegiance to an ideal,
Pledged all my honour and my zeal.
I learned the ropes, the bombs, the guns,
I joined with Ireland's risen ones.
I took my place beside the others
Bright-eyed friends, sisters, brothers
Rallied now with grit and pride
Standing there at Ireland's side.
Until the day they put me down
On a bloody street in my home town.
My rifle hot, my bullets spent
I fought the fight by my intent.
Then the cortège, flag-draped, proud,
They harass, pummel, flank and crowd.
I was a soldier stern and gave my life
In this ragged post-colonial strife
But know me now and the cause I served.
Acknowledge this, as I deserve.

It's okay. Just the infections. Gives me a high
temperature. Under control. Under control.

Scene 3

You must be joking. Who's going to stand up and say that
the truth of the past is that he was a soldier? Who's going to
say that? (*Beat*.) Apart from his family, his neighbours and
his comrades? (*Beat, thinks*.) A good number of people.

I know stuff like that needs dealt with.

Scared? You try being brave with the voices of the dead raging in your head. You try skipping and hopping at the thought of having the truth cut out of you. 'Course I'm scared.

I should be okay about it. I've had bits of it looked at already. The odd inquiry. Stuff buried in my spleen. I got a pile of information; yeh, no doubt about that. But the truth?

I know. I know. I was one of the loudest clamouring for it. We're all born free and equal, I said. We're all equal before the law. Who did it? Who pulled the trigger? Who gave the order? Who buried the file? It's complicated, because the dead are all equally dead but, in their dying, are they equivalent?

And the dead are crowding round me now.

I'm scared, yeh, but I do want to lance the boil, plunge the scalpel in and gouge the poison out. The dead have infected me. All the dead. Over three and half thousand of them. I'm well infected I am.

He looks up as if he hears voices around him.

Please. Why me?

The dead abound, the dead abound.
The truth cries out, the truth cries out.
How do we still that urgent shout?

Do you want truth?

A spasm of pain hits him.

I'm a son of the soil from Lancashire,
Wondering how I got to be here.
I'm know I'm supposed to defend the realm,
But I have some doubts about the men at the helm.
You see I joined up under economic duress
And I didn't expect it to be such a mess.
I should be at home eating hotpots
Instead of guarding this border and ducking potshots.
I have some respect for the ones out there taking them
I mean they're volunteers, nobody's forcing them,
But what if one gets real lucky, has a go and hits?
There's not much 'land of hope and glory' about this Blitz.
No one in Westminster will stand up and take it,
They'll duck and dive and bob and weave and fake it.
I mean, does my truth have any rights
Now the potshot has come in and shut down my lights?

No. No worries. I'm fine. A wee turn, that's all. But, I ask
you, would you go through with it? (*Beat.*) You see my
position.

Scene 4

Pain? Of course there's pain. It's consuming me.
Supposing I did go through with it tomorrow, would the
pain lift? Everything taken out and then I'm pain-free? I
tell you one thing. I'm terrified I'll be worse off. I know
there's no cure for this. A set of procedures and that's
it? 'Course not. I'm petrified I'll be hurt by all this truth
recovery.

Maybe it would make me better. (*Beat.*) Maybe it would
make me worse. Would it make me stable? All I really
want is stability. Do I want peace? What the hell is peace?
I just want stability.

I suppose if I went through with it at least I'd have
the records. The files. The testimonies. The witness
statements. The full facts. The knowledge. No disputes. No
queries. Comprehensive. It's only when you really know
something that you can put it behind you. (*Beat.*) Right?

Then maybe I could say, Danny boy, you brought the dead
close to you. And you survived. All the dead. The soldiers,
the civilians, the volunteers, the comrades, the guilty, the
innocent, the malign, the benign, the yours, the mine.

Pause.

Things would come out that were better left buried,
wouldn't they?

If I open my innards to this truth recovery and let the world
listen to the thrum of blood in my heart, the gush of bile
in my spleen, the susurrations of air in my lungs, the drip,
drip, drip of urine in my kidneys, the clatter of corpuscles
and platelets in my arteries, when I sound them all from
deep inside where the dead reside, will I be healed?

'Course I'm weak from it. Weakened by it. What do you
expect?

I know I have a right to a fair and public hearing that is
independent and impartial. I'm not stupid. And I say there
has to be a form. Procedures. Terms of reference. Who
set up the Panel? Who's paying for it? Who's on it? Who
benefits from it? You can't just dive in any old way, poke
among my innards, pick out one juicy morsel of tripe and
suck the truth out of it willy-nilly.

It's the records I want. Give me the records. The
knowledge. The who, the why, the where, the when and
the what happened? Simple enough questions.

Pick one. Go on. Pick any part of me. The thigh? The
shoulder? The belly? The heart? Ah! The heart! Go on.
Pick one. Take yourself back to 1969. The year I was
born. To the very start of it all. Then run with time's
arrow from 1969, and all the way through the murderous
Seventies and into the pitch-dark Eighties then on again
into the stuttering Nineties. Right up to now. That's
it. Focus on the dead now. The memory of the dead.
The ones who died violently. And ask yourself these
questions. Who? Why? They're the killer ones. When?
Where? Maybe those two are easy enough. Maybe even
'What happened?' is doable. I'll give you a minute. I
need a rest.

Sits. Pause.

You have some of the answers. Maybe even all of the
answers. What's missing? (*Beat.*) I know. What's missing
is the person. The person. The person is missing. And
the truth. What's missing is the truth. Knowledge is one
thing. Truth is something else.

Pause. Stands.

I just want someone to stand up and raise his or her hand.
You remember, like we used to do in school, when we
wanted to go to the toilet?

Something intimate and revelatory like that. Just stand
up, hold up their hand and say:
Excuse me.
Yes, that's it, nice and slowly now, so we can all hear.
Excuse me.
Lovely.
Excuse me, but…
Ah!

Excuse me, but I…
Yes?
Excuse me, but I did it.

Is that it? Is that what all this is about? A mound of knowledge, then admissions? Will that cure me? Take the sting out of all of this and put the record straight when we hear it cried out – I did it.

I shot, I bombed, I raided, I shredded, I disappeared, I planned, I colluded, I orchestrated, I planted, I targeted, I informed, and I ordered it.

I'll be going through this truth recovery for a long time.

Okay, so you did it. What now? (*Beat.*) You want to say you're sorry?

He looks up as if he hears voices around him.

No! Not now. No! Please!

The dead abound, the dead abound.
How do we keep them in the ground?

You want prosecutions?

A spasm of pain hits him.

Drive by, drive by,
Scatter shot flying.
Pool of blood,
Is that me dying?
Drive by, drive by,
Stop and count.
I rise up now

And seek account.
Feud, feud, feud, feud.
The whole bloody thing got screwed.
Take him out, wrong three letters.
What's this? Insults his betters?
Used to be comrades, Red Hands linking
Always loyal, never thinking
The change would come and I'd be Other,
Victim of my own brother.
Feud, feud, feud, feud.
The whole bloody thing got screwed.
Take him out, wrong three letters.
What's this? Insults his betters?
Oh! Some did well with their flashy cars
And some did time behind prison bars.
Me? I fester in the ground
And watch the latest burl-around.
Feud, feud, feud, feud.
The whole bloody thing got screwed.
Take him out, wrong three letters.
What's this? Insults his betters?

Stand up and say it.
Put the cards upon the table.
As Cain lives so I was Abel.
That much I ask so I can rest
Among the ranks of Ulster's blessed.

It's okay. I'll be fine. A visitation, you could say. I'm fine.

Scene 5

Prosecutions? Could be inevitable. I'm not making any
predictions.

You know as well as I do that apologies mean nothing unless they mean making sure it doesn't happen again. Unless you can say you'll endeavour – no, not endeavour – ensure – that's it, ensure – that it never happens again, then keep your sorry. Your sorry is no good to me.

But stand there now and hold your hand up. That's it.
Repeat it.
Excuse me, but I did it. And I'm sorry.
Good. Go on.
I was wrong.
Be specific.
I did it and I was wrong.
Did what?
You know.
Spell it out.

That's what they want me to do tomorrow. Spell it out.
Spill it out. (*Beat.*) No way.

You're surprised there's no one here except me. But, then again, any one of you could be where I am. We've all got it inside us. The truth of the past.

So don't ask me to do it on my own. Don't ask me to do the truth recovery while you stand on the sidelines muttering 'get on with it'. (*Laughs and points at audience member.*) I knew that thought had crossed your mind.

It could be any one of us.

Yes, you. (*Points at audience members.*) Does your heart ache with the truth of the past? Do your joints creak at the pain of memories? Do your body cavities throb at the unsolved murders, the lost files, the buried remains in the bog? My very being shudders with it all.

94

I know. You've said it before. I take it on too much.
Daniel, you said, let it go. Move on, Danny. Yes, people
do bad things to other people, but it's in the past.

I am trying to let it go. I am trying to prise its steely fingers
from around my neck, one by bitter one, lift the nails out
of the flesh, prise back the knuckles, loosen the wrist and
unclamp the grip. So I can breathe my fullest again.

I know. I know. You always took a different view from
me on this. You said that if we go back into it we'll only
disturb it. Best to let the Lion sleep you said. Don't go
there you said because when you go down into the blood
sludge and stir your truth recovery into it all, you'll only
make it worse. You'll only waken the Lions of hate and
arrogance who lurk there and you'll give them the light
they need to flourish and ravage once more. And this time
they'll ravage our children.

He looks up as if he hears voices around him.

Will you never let me be?

The dead abound, the dead abound.
How do we keep them in the ground?
The truth cries out, the truth cries out.
How do we still that urgent shout?

You want justice?

A spasm of pain hits him.

Wrong place, wrong time.
Your place, not mine.
Take this, take that.
Rock, bar, brick, bat.

Waste ground, no frills.
Bust head, hate kills.
Last breath, faint cry.
No hope, just die.
No more, last one.
What's done is done.
Come clean, call time
On war and crime.
Say that it's true
That is my due.

It's okay. No worries. They come to me, that's all. I'll be
fine.

Scene 6

You're right. How can we ever get to the truth of the
past when we can't even agree on what the past was?
Is. (*Beat.*) I think I'm going to have to go back on
the cigarettes. I gave them up. About a fortnight now.
Doing the patches and all. (*Laughs.*) No, it's not part
of the preparation for this. If you thought giving up the
cigarettes was bad, wait till you start the truth recovery.
You haven't one on you by any chance? No. Better not.
Only a step backwards. Have to keep on keeping on. As
the song says.

Some of it hurts more than others. 'Course it does. And
the Panel – they just tell me to stay calm.

I am calm.
You're not calm, Danny.
Calm as can be. Cool as a cucumber.
You're not calm, Danny.
I am calm. And I'll tell you how calm I am. I can look

you straight in the eye and say I want my tax money back. Don't tell me you have no money for these procedures, when you spent my taxes killing fellow citizens.

I am calm. Drugs? 'Course I'm on drugs. It's the twenty-first century, isn't it?

I do want the wrongdoers brought to book. Certainly brought to book. Called to account.

Swear on the Bible. Swear, swear, and swear. Swear to tell the whole truth and nothing but the truth, so help me I will, I will, so, help me, please help me, because I'm melting in this. I'm a wax man burning from the inside out.

Danny boy, the pipes, the pipes ...'tis you, 'tis you must rise. Rise, I say, and take me to where I can find rest and ease.

Yes, I know we're not going to get at everything. But at least enough to make a difference overall. Can I at least try for that?

He looks up as if he hears voices around him.

Once more, I beg you, leave me be!

The dead abound, the dead abound.
How do we keep them in the ground?

Is it revenge you want?

A spasm of pain hits him.

With rolling thunder, shattering glass
The brimstone claimed me in one pass.
My clothes, my flesh were all consumed.
A flaming stench the world perfumed.
And stronger still the smell of Time
That layered itself upon the crime,
Till now it lingers over all
In wisps of smoke that rise and fall
To cover up the wrong was done
And blind the eyes of everyone.
But if the truth it be made clear
Then I will take my rest right here.
I want a solid cure forever
That this fiery pass of brimstone never
More will in this place be found.
Acknowledge this and I'll stay in the ground.

No worries. I'm fine. No, just a spasm.

Of course I'm calm. Calm, but not cold.

Scene 7

Sometimes they go on at me to tell stories. Tell us,
Daniel. We promise not to doze off. Tell us a story. A
good deep one, full of anguish, blood and broken people.
Oh, the more gory the better.

And I tell them one. I go into it. The details. (*Beat.*) The
tyre marks on the road. Footsteps. The lights. Gone. A
broken cup. Great darkness. Then, too soon, a hearse
puffing grey exhaust fumes. My feet. Shuffling. Pills
shaped like torpedoes. Tremors in the glass of water in
my hand.

I tell them everything. All the scraps I know. And for a while I feel good. There's a raw place where I dug it all out. They dug it out really. Gave me the scalpels. A raw place, still oozing pus and blood. Then that dulls a little and a scab forms. Blood toughens and builds itself into a plug. And it holds there. Later a throb grows. A dull thump rises to the steady hum of something not properly addressed.

And they say, that's good, Danny. You told your story. And we heard you. That's good, Danny. Have a rest now. Rest now. You'll feel better after a rest.

Pause.

Except I don't. When I come to, I sense it. I've told the story, so I feel different. But do I feel better? I know I feel vulnerable. Because now, so many more people know the details of the past within me. So many more people know me as victim. And what have I gained? It has to be more than just telling stories. It has to be.

No, we're not all victims. Some people did things. Some people had things done to them. Some people, well, they're a bit of both. There you have it. Three options.

Option A. I did things. No doubts. No arguments. Option B. Things were done to me. What do you mean it's not clear? (*Laughs.*) 'Course it's not clear.

The truth of the past. Violence. Death. Wrongs. Option A. You did it. Option B. It was done to you. Option C? Option C is a combination of A and B.

Option D? What? Option D? Right. You're just there and you're wondering what all the fuss is about? Yeh, you

know there was bother. Trouble even. You saw it on the
telly, but you got used to switching it off. You got away
to the sun for as long as you could when the summer
madness took off.

I don't know what to do about Option D.

All I'm saying is we're not all victims and we're not all
perpetrators and I have to see how the truth of the past
affects me. And if I want to go into it, let it be because I
want to survive. I don't want to wallow in it all the rest of
my days and be a burdensome, bothersome old man who
spilled his past into the future and spoiled it.

I'm not innocent. I'm not naïve. I've seen a thing or two.
Done a thing or two. Option C. And I'm angry, too.

(*Agitated.*) Oh! Danny boy, the pipes, the pipes, the pipes,
the pipes, the pipes.

Did none of you bring grapes? Isn't that what you're
supposed to do? Bring grapes. Or a bottle of Lucozade?
Did none of you even think to smuggle me in a drink?
Ah, don't worry about it. Can't have it anyway. Have to
be sober for this.

I went into the Panel and I said, hold your horses. Grab
the reins there, pardners. Let's get the politics sorted out
first. Get the old guns and government stuff in the bag
before we go down the truth recovery road.

They didn't like that. They want the whole thing over and
done with. And so do I, but the problem is our past is not
like anywhere else. We're at a kind of jagged stalemate
here. It must be the longest endgame in the world. No
check. No checkmate. Just stale, stale, stale. (*Beat.*) Mate.

We start throwing truth recovery in among all that and
who knows where it could go. Boom! Boom! Ka-boom!
Check and mate and goodbye, Danny boy! See you again
in another thirty-odd years.

Forget about it? Is that what you want me to do? Just
forget about it. Just let the past wander off somewhere
and get lost in the woods, so we can all forget about it.

Until the day the children come running out of the trees,
their eyes bulging, their teeth chattering, their little hearts
jumping out of their chests, screaming Lion! Lion! Lion!
The dead abound! The Lion is awake!

The Lion is awake and he's dripping wrongs and
memories and he's yowling for vengeance and he's
picking up the children in mouthfuls and tossing them
this way and that, so that they turn one upon another in
their panic and begin to maul and wreck and trample,
hurt and beat each other and once more *they* become the
Lion and it's as if we, you and me, never lived at all.
Never hoped that our lives could be better. Never said to
ourselves, let's get things sorted. Once and for all.

They must be off their heads if they think I'm going to go
through with it. They can't force me. No one can. I won't
participate.

Pause.

I know. The complications. And the children. I keep
coming back to them. The children.

He looks up as if he hears voices around him.

Will you not give me peace?

The dead abound, the dead, the dead, the dead, the dead, the dead.

A spasm of pain hits him.

I expected more.
They're supposed to be professionals, upholding the law.
They shot me down with it.
Here's your law and order.
Rat-tat tat-tat tat.

They lied about me.
They said I had a rifle, loaded and cocked.
So they had to fire at me
As an act of self-defence.
Rat-tat tat-tat tat.

I had no rifle.
Twenty years old, an upright working man.
I paid taxes.
I paid for the bullet that killed me.
Rat-tat tat-tat tat.

They proved nothing.
Just made claims, shut up shop and got on with it.
Closed ranks, closed the file.
Kept doing it.
Rat-tat tat-tat tat.

So what now, then?
It was thirty-odd years ago, too late to uncover.
The forensics were negative.
The moths ate the file.
Rat-tat tat-tat tat.

Someone should stand up.
Someone needs to say it was wrong, all those years ago.

Say it won't happen again
Even though it does.
Rat-tat tat-tat tat.

Not just anyone.
I mean top dogs, people with position and power.
Who have the file and the law.
You know who I mean.
Rat-tat tat-tat tat.

Okay. I'm fine. The restless dead are with us. (*Beat.*) Just give me a second.

Scene 8

I'm glad you came. You've made me reconsider. The dead deserve the respect. I know that. But I won't be having the truth cut out of me for them. If I do it, I'll be doing it for the children. So they won't have to. So the record can be made and set in stone. Gravestones. Tombstones. Milestones of history that are behind us.

Who am I kidding? (*Laughs.*) Acting like I've got it all worked out. Acting like I'm as right as rain about this whole truth recovery process. I am not. But I will go under it. Some day. And in a whole variety of ways. Because if what this is about is closure – this being the end of the thing – then I want to be sure they get it all. So I can survive. Scarred, seared, battered, red raw and ravaged. Show my face. Call my name. Daniel. Out of the Lion's den. Daniel. Oh! Danny, Danny boy.

Sings.

Oh! Danny boy, the pipes, the pipes are calling
From glen to glen and down the mountainside.

The summers gone, and all the roses falling,
'Tis you, 'tis you must go and I must bide.
But come ye back… (*Breaks down.*)

Speaks.

But come ye back.
No, it's okay. I know the dead are never coming back. I
never could manage the high notes.
'Tis I'll be here. In sunshine or in shadow.
Oh! Danny boy, the pipes, the pipes, the pipes, the pipes
indeed.
And the winter hushed and white with snow, covering us
all in a blanket I will lift, if only to let in a feeble light.

Can you hear them? The gentle dead? Never coming back.

Okay, I'll talk to the Panel again tomorrow. I'll tell them
that we've had this chat. Best to keep them informed. Keep
everybody on board as they say. Yeh. Let's try to get some
sleep and then in the morning, we'll see. Because, you
know, it'll be different in the morning. We'll all be stronger.
For facing the past full-on, so our children can have their
future. They'll have their own hurts, but let's be honest
now, we don't want to bequeath this stuff to them, do we?

(*Gets up to leave.*) No. No need. I'll make it all right.
Thanks for coming to visit.
Yeh.
I'll talk to you tomorrow.
Yeh.
Tomorrow.

Danny *leaves.*

Scenes from an Inquiry

No. 1 A Cartography

Counsel You say you heard the shot while you were in the van?

Witness Yes.

Counsel Did you get out then?

Witness Yes.

Counsel And would you say the shot came from the east?

Witness I'm not sure.

Counsel (*To technicians.*) Can we have map M104.3 on the screen? Thank you. (*To* **Witness**.) You said you were near the junction of William Street and Rossville Street? Did the shot come from the east of this position?

Witness The sun rises in the east. I know it comes up over the park and the river and, if there's no fog, we see it.

Counsel Quite.

Witness Then it rises above the city, crosses The Diamond and heads out the river before vanishing behind low hills.

Counsel In the west?

Witness Between Creggan and Killea. Your map doesn't stretch over the ground. It doesn't contour into the spaces, the hollows, the crevices and humps that make a city.

Judge Counsel is simply trying to establish your exact location.

Counsel Can we take you back to the map?

Witness Yes, but you can't take me back to the streets. The day. The sights and the smells. The way people gathered. Ran. Stood amazed. The way a horror flowed out like a delta.

Counsel You say you heard three shots? Can we locate them?

Witness Memory can't be flattened out by pointing. It has dimensions in time and space. Your maps are for spreading on big tables and neat screens. Your maps have no depth. No mud. No fear. No blood.

Counsel I'd like to take you back to the barricade. The one you said in your statement you passed earlier in the morning.

Witness The sun hadn't risen then. It was dark in the east. The west. The north and the south.

Counsel (*To technicians.*) Can we have photograph P1078? Can we have some light?

No. 2 An Espionage

Counsel My Lord, the search for truth is utmost in our minds.

Judge Of course. It is a sacred search.

Counsel As sacred as life itself.

Judge Of course.

Witness Can I say something here?

Counsel We have an interest in both, my Lord. In truth and in life. The nation has an interest in both. It is a national interest.

Witness What about my interest?

Judge Your point if you may, Counsel?

Counsel My point, my Lord, is that we must serve the national interest in order to serve both truth and life. If we do not serve the national interest we will threaten truth and life.

Judge And we don't want to do that.

Witness Sounds to me like you're serving yourselves.

Counsel No, we don't want to do that. So this evidence must not be presented in public. In the interest of truth and life. In the national interest.

Judge It's a good point.

Counsel I thought you'd like it.

Witness What about the public interest? Is this a public inquiry or what? We're not heading for another whitewash are we?

Judge I think perhaps we should rise for lunch.

Witness What about the truth, the whole truth and nothing but the truth, so help me…

Judge To lunch.

Counsel Perhaps an early lunch would be a good idea.

No. 3 A Refuge

Counsel You say you ran.

Witness What do you expect? They were firing live rounds. Everybody ran.

Counsel Where did you run?

Witness For cover. I ran for cover. I left a boy behind me. We all did. We all ran for cover. Over the low wall.

Counsel A wall. (*To technicians.*) Can we have photograph P132, please?

Witness Just a wall. A low wall. Barely enough to cover us.

Counsel And what did you find there?

Witness Huddled bodies panting. A woman missing a shoe. A boy crying. His friend holding his hand. Woodlice scurrying because we'd disturbed them.

Counsel Can I ask you to look at the photograph? Thank you. Is this the wall?

Witness It seemed bigger. Like the Great Wall of China. Or the Berlin Wall. It was huge. It had to be. It stood between me and the grave.

Counsel (*To technicians.*) Can we zoom in on the lower part of the photograph, please? Thank you. (*To* **Witness**.) Is that you, in the lower right-hand corner?

Witness I seem so small, no bigger than a woodlice.

Judge If you would be so kind as to say whether you recognise yourself?

Witness I look at the photograph and I see myself, but it's not me. I see a refugee, you know, like you see climbing out of the back of cargo trailers at Dover. Boxed in for days, they stagger out blinking and skinny, not knowing where they are.

Counsel You were behind the low wall.

Witness I never wanted to leave that place. I never felt so scared and yet so safe. I knew that it was the safest place on earth. Down among the woodlice. With the boy crying. And the woman with the one shoe. Refugees, wanting a home.

Counsel (*To technicians.*) Can we zoom in some more, please?

No. 4 A Wrong Number

Counsel Can I ask you to look at this photograph now? You see the group behind the phone box? Do you recognise anyone?

Witness One man had his hands in the air. Like a goalie.

Counsel Which man?

Witness One minute he was with us. The next he was gone.

Counsel (*To technicians.*) Can we lighten the photograph, please?

Witness I saw three dead that day. Hardest counting I ever did. I was scared I'd get the wrong number. But I didn't know the half of it. Found that out later.

Counsel If you…

Witness Funny, I was always good with numbers. Say your phone number once and I've got it. Go on, try me.

Judge I really don't think…

Witness Ach, don't bother, then. You've probably got a big long rigmarole of a mobile number anyway. Make a difference if it was to happen now. We'd all have mobile phones. We were so young. We'd all be dialling and texting away. All across the world.

Judge Do you really think that would make a difference?

Witness Why? It's not going to happen again, is it?

Counsel If I could ask you about the phone box…

Witness That's why they call it the web. We were caught in a web. Trying to find a corner to hide in. Like we were queuing to make a call. Except the phone box was red. Red for danger. None of us had a mobile. We were frozen. None of us had the number.

Counsel I'm not sure if we should concentrate so much on the arithmetic.

Witness Why not? Thirteen shot dead. Fifteen wounded and injured. There's arithmetic for you. One-three. One-five. Two-eight. Could be a phone number. Something you'd dial and it would ring out all over the world. Ring and ring and ring and keep on ringing until somebody, somebody answered.

Judge Can you please try to answer the Counsel's questions?

Witness Does he have my number?

Counsel Can we take you back to the photograph?

No. 5 A Library

Counsel I put it to you that you don't remember any of this. I put it to you that you read all this in a book.

Witness I read all the books. All the articles.

Counsel And they influenced you so that you can't tell the difference now between what you know and what you remember.

Witness I have a shelf in the back room. It used to have weans' books on it, but they're all grown up. I put me own books there now. McCann's. Mullan's. Bishop Daly's. The Insight Team. Videos, too. Docu-dramas. TV films. Jimmy McGovern. Jimmy Nesbitt. A shelf full.

Judge Is that not somewhat obsessive?

Witness You're an educated man. Probably read a few books in your day. Things are solid in books. You see, when you're told at that age – remember I was seventeen, an impressionable age – and when the impression is impressed upon you that it never happened, that it was nothing at all like you remember it, well, you know, doubts set in. So you go in search of knowledge. And books, well, books are solid.

Counsel Yes, but what I think we're trying to arrive at here, is whether it is possible you don't remember any of this. It's possible you just know it from a book.

Witness You telling me I shouldn't read? You want me ignorant?

Judge No, not at all. Counsel is not suggesting that…

Witness There's memory and knowledge. I have both. Books are a scaffolding. I'm trying to be fair. I read. I climbed. I looked down. I remembered.

Counsel Can we ask you to have a look at an extract from one of those books? (*To technicians.*) Can we have E221, please? Thank you.

No. 6 An Episcopacy

Counsel You later took up the crozier?

Witness Much later.

Judge At that time you were simply a priest?

Witness Nothing simple about it. Home visits, the rituals of birth, marriage and death. Pastimes, too. I did quite a lot of shows and amateur dramatics in those days.

For a long time after that day I could have played Lady Macbeth. You know the lines: 'Out, damned spot!'?

Counsel I do indeed. Would you say you were a rallying point?

Witness It was only a handkerchief. I never meant it as a flag. I was rallying sinners. I was shepherding a shoal of humanity around a corner into the lens of a camera.

Judge The Lord is your shepherd, then?

Witness The Lord is my shepherd. There is not a thing that I shall want. Except perhaps to bring that day back and start all over again. Never have to wave a handkerchief. Never have to lean over a boy and breathe the rituals of death into his ear as the life goes out of him.

Judge I've always loved the psalms. We're trying to walk the paths of righteousness here you know.

Witness We walked through the valley of death that day. Ghosts walk with me still.

Counsel Are you not afraid of them?

Witness No, not at all. There is goodness and mercy if we can find it. It takes time. A long time. Some people grow impatient.

Counsel You?

Witness I will fear no evil. Not since that day. And I will dwell in the house of the Lord, with the boy whose last breath rushed past me into the darkening air.

Counsel Might I ask you to look at a photograph?

No. 7 A Bestiary

Counsel Surely you can't ask us to believe you saw a...
a... gorgon?

Witness Lots of them. Belching fire. And fury. And
five-headed mastiffs, big as jet bombers. I still see them.
Cerberus out front, so awful that when he came towards
us we all froze. He spat at us and poison burned the air.

Counsel My Lord, these are myths.

Witness And Balor strode among us that day, put the evil
eye on all of us. Took the breath of all of us. Took the life
of some of us. Ravaged our heels. Scattered us, a herd
of red deer flying over the hillside, our feet dragging and
sluggish in the heather of our fear.

Counsel My Lord, I must ask you...

Witness Centaurs trampled the streets, hurling bolts of
lightning. Werewolves big as aircraft carriers slabbered
over us. Eagles clawed at our hair and at our skin. I
saw a woman fall and be lifted up and tossed away by a
mastodon. I see her still.

Judge If I may? Counsel has already referred to your
1972 statement in which you mention Basilisks. Would
you care to...

Witness All they have to do is look at you. They came in
armoured vehicles and got down on one knee, half bird,
with luminous feathers, half reptile, with gangrous scales.
And they looked at us. 'Don't look back,' I shouted, but
some did and they were felled by the glares.

Counsel Some of the language is a bit too colourful. I mean, how can we ever get to the truth of it?

Judge We have to accept the language we're given. I mean we talk about 'pigs', don't we?

Witness There were pigs, wild boars, grunting, snorting and roaring over the waste ground towards the flats.

Counsel At last, something we can deal with. Waste ground. Can I ask you to look at this photograph, please?

No. 8 A Specimen

Counsel What we do is we put things on to a slide. A thin sliver of a thing, the most minute, ångström-wide slice, then we slap it under a microscope and we look through it. Not just at it. Right through it.

Witness Sounds like a medical act to me. Like bodies being tossed into the back of a vehicle. A medical act, with the stench of the abattoir about it.

Judge We see the constituent parts, the inner forms, the whorls, the wheels and wiggles that comprise the thing. We see the light.

Witness But only at the cost of making specimens of us. You treat us as so much plant life. So many specimens to be plucked and dissected. So many slides to be looked right through.

Counsel You say you saw three bodies being put into the back of the vehicle.

Witness Yes. Three. Three specimens you might say.

Judge I don't think Counsel would put it quite that way.

Witness No matter what way you put it, it was gross. I've worked in a butcher's shop. I've seen blood dripping off meat.

Counsel It would be better if we stayed with the facts.

Witness The facts are that butchers have more savvy. They don't look right through things. They have more respect. That's what was missing. Respect. That's the truth of it.

Counsel Can I ask you to look at hotspot H719, please?

No. 9 A Glorious Knight

Counsel You showed great courage in standing up to the soldiers…

Judge I agree.

Counsel … but wasn't it somewhat foolhardy?

Witness That's me all right. The hardy fool. From the moment I was born I was standing up. I was walking at eight months. I rode a bicycle when I was three. When my brother fell and cried over his scratched knee I wiped him clean with the end of my skirt. Nose. Eyes. Knee. And he smiled and ran off.

Counsel You were not a qualified nurse. You were simply a Knight…

Judge In shining armour… sorry… couldn't resist… sorry.

Witness I was a Knight of Malta.

Counsel It's a small island.

Witness Like our own.

Counsel You were a small woman. A girl.

Judge A brave girl. Showed great courage under fire.

Witness What did you expect me to do? Run away? Boys were getting shot. They needed help. Everyone was flat on their faces. I was standing. In my white coat, with my little bag of bandages and creams and my hair tied back in a ponytail to keep it out of my face. Because I knew I'd need to show my face that day.

Counsel Soldiers threatened you.

Witness I threatened them. Yes, they pointed their guns at me. Yes, they took aim. But I took aim, too.

Judge You were armed?

Witness I took aim with my eyes. I was armed with my anger and my heart. And my wee bag of bandages and creams. So the soldiers turned and slouched away and I went to the boys. If only I had that old skirt I had when I was a girl. That miracle skirt that could clean a boy's wounds so he could get up and run away smiling. That old skirt with the pleats squished out of it and the jaggedy lemonade stain like an island.

Counsel You gave first aid.

Witness I was first there. What aid I gave was minimal. I prayed. I cried.

Counsel I wonder if I could ask you to take a look at a photograph? (*To technicians.*) Could we have photograph P387, please?

No. 10 A Rockery

Counsel If we could swing around a little to the left, you will see roughly where you were standing.

Witness Forget about your maps and your photos and your hotspots. Show me some of the stones we threw that day. Build me something with them.

Counsel The stones are long gone.

Witness They are not. Stones don't go away. Stones and rocks stay. People go. Or get swept up. Or move on. I am the wife of such a man. He threw stones once. Now he swings a trowel. We studied stones together. Knew their heft and form, their composition and content. He told me how they materialised from the ground. I told him we lived on rocky ground. Our lives are rubble, I said. I've been building ever since. A life. A family. Building Lego with the babies. He's been building, too.

Judge We'd like to bring you back to the day itself. Perhaps a map would help.

Counsel Can you look at this map, please? (*To technicians.*) Map M45.22, please. The lower section only. That's where you met your husband.

Witness At the rubble barricade. Pavers, halvers, lumps of concrete, random pebbles and roly-poly stones like you'd find on a beach. We crouched. We studied rocks. I lifted one and hurled it. It arced high in the air and landed among others. Still as love. Permanent as hope. Solid as defiance. And then the stones caught fire.

Counsel Was this at the barricade? If you take control of the pointer, can you indicate where you and your future husband met?

Witness We met in the rubble, in the midst of the stones. We threw them and then we fashioned our lives from them. We are masons, brickies, sculptors, gardeners. We put roses among the rocks, drew lilies through the concrete.

Counsel Perhaps we need a photograph.

No. 11 A Reliquary

Counsel I know this is difficult for you. But if you could just try to answer the questions. If you need a break…

Witness It's okay. I'll go on.

Judge You were talking about a box.

Witness We had a box in the attic. Not a very big box. And the attic is as cold as the grave. Come the day I couldn't get up there any more, they took the box down for me, to keep in the wardrobe. The dust tried to cover it, but I brushed it off. The dust is covering him and that's too much. So I wouldn't let it near the box.

Counsel We're trying to find out…

Witness It didn't take much cleaning ever. I have a wee cloth I keep special for it. It's a holy thing. I mean, to me. We all have boxes like that in the house. You probably have one, too. Something you lost. Something taken from you. You find a box to put things in, so you can hold onto them. A medal, a broken watch, photos, a piece of a shirt. Only a wee piece because it's only a wee box. Sometimes I sit on me own up in the room with the box on me knees and I look out the window. The starlings gather and fly off. The light leaves the sky. The box stays on my knees. I dust off the tears, one by one.

Counsel Perhaps we should take a break.

No. 12 A Cacophony

Counsel (*To technicians.*) Can we have photograph P993, please? Thank you. (*To* **Witness**.) Can you hear me?

Witness I wear a hearing aid now. An implant. But that day, everything was crystal. Even now with the hearing aid out, I can sometimes hear the woman calling.

Judge I thought you said it was a man?

Witness There was a woman calling, too. She was above me, at a window in the flats. 'Don't go out,' she called. 'Don't go out. Stay where you are.'

Counsel And can we just clarify… can you hear me all right?

Witness Yes.

Counsel Can we just clarify where exactly you were at that moment?

Witness I was in the alley. The man was crouching out by the wall. Hands and knees. Crawling. Then on his belly. His voice calling.

Counsel Could you make out what he was saying?

Witness The alley was like an echo chamber. The bullets whooshed and whizzed around. And a blackbird perched on the roof of a shed singing like it was Christmas. The blackbird, and the man calling out. Two dogs started answering each other back, one bark upon another. A lorry… sounded like a lorry… revving up. Feet running all over the place like water rushing down a gravelly banking. And always the voice of the man. Calling.

Counsel You went out to the man.

Witness There was a lull. Not a lull. A hush. Just the briefest of hushes, as if God put a finger to his lips and went ssssh! Then maybe he took it away, because it all began again. Birds, lorries, feet, dogs. Bullets. And the man calling. So I crouched down and went to him.

Counsel Is that you, in the photograph, crouched down?

Witness I've seen that photograph many times before.

Judge Can you please confirm that the crouching figure is you?

Witness The photo is so mute. It doesn't tell the half of it. The sound of it.

Counsel Can you say if that is you?

Witness I can say this. I was deafened that day. Sound never worked for me after that. Yes, it is me. A version of me. I recognise the coat. The way my hair was. That look in my eye. But I'm not sure I can hear the man calling.

Counsel I don't think we have audio of that, my Lord. Never get it separated out from everything else. Perhaps if we zoom in on the figure in the photo?

No. 13 A Video Link

Counsel This is most unsatisfactory. Someone has remote control and we can't seem to get a link.

Judge Try them again.

Counsel Are you there? Can you see anything?

Witness What? I saw nothing. There were crowds of people. The whole thing was mad. Crazy. But we were professional. It's what we're trained for.

Judge I'm not getting anything. Is there a technical hitch?

Counsel Hello? Can you hear anything?

Witness What? I heard nothing. Just my orders. Round up the hooligans. Get the yobos. That's what we did.

Judge I'm still not getting anything.

Counsel (*To technicians.*) The link seems to be down. Can somebody do something?

No. 14 A Lament

Counsel Is there anything else you remember?

Witness All of a sudden, all of a sudden I heard singing.
I wasn't sure. I thought it was a radio. But then I knew it
was a voice. A woman's voice. My sister. From high up in
the flats. Like a blackbird. Sweet and high up.

Sings.

As all the streets below me clear,
I search for him that I hold dear.
And still I know he's gone away
And left me on this bloody day.

The clouds come in to close the world
And darken the eyes of this girl.
It is the end of this bloody day
And my bright boy has gone away.

But light shall shine, I know it will
And I will hold it high until
The truth reveals this bloody day
When my sweet love, he went away.

All

All you who are of good intent
On truth and justice be you bent.
So all the world may with us say,
We made peace with that bloody day.

The Saville Inquiry
London Scenarios

Scenario 1
Going into Central Hall

Protesters, Father, Daughter.

A loud and aggressive group of **Protesters** *line the entrance to the Methodist Central Hall, London. They spit, chant and jeer, shaking their placards: JUSTICE FOR THE PARAS, SUPPORT OUR BOYS.*

Protesters Go home! Go home! Go home! Should have shot more of you! Fenian scum! Irish bastards! Cunts! Go, Paras! Go, Paras! Go, Paras! Go!

Father It's all right, daughter. It's all right.

Daughter Is there no other way in, Daddy?

Father We're going in the front door. Just ignore them.

Daughter Why did we have to come over anyway? Why couldn't Saville have stayed in Derry?

Father Look, we're sticking with this even if they move it to Timbuktu. We're not backing out now. That's what they want.

Daughter Right, Daddy. 'Mon ahead.

Protesters *chant.*

Protester (*Shooting action.*) They didn't shoot enough of you.

Daughter How can you say that? You don't know what you're talking about.

Father It's okay. Just ignore them. Come on. Come on.

Protester Fuck off home, you cunt.

Father Watch your language, you.

Daughter Who do you think you're talking to?

Protester Go, Paras! Go! Go, Paras! Go! Go, Paras! Go!

Crowd picks it up. **Father** *lunges at* **Protester**.

Daughter (*Scream.*) Daddy!

She grabs him from the scuffle and leads him on.

Father (*Under his breath.*) Bastards.

Father *and* **Daughter** *go through entrance arch.*
Protesters *chant and then move off through audience.*

Scenario 2
Inside Central Hall

Lawyer, Soldier, Brother 1, Brother 2, Father, Daughter.

Lawyer You say in your statement, and I'm quoting here, that you came under a hail of gunfire.

Soldier That's right.

Lawyer Could you estimate the number of shots?

Soldier Hard to say. Hundreds.

Brother 1 Thousands.

Lawyer This was when you were on the waste ground.

Soldier Yeh, soon as we got out of the vehicles.

Brother 1 Bastards tried to mow you down.

Lawyer Can I ask you to look at photograph P974, please. Thank you.

Soldier No problem, Miss.

Lawyer Is that you beside the vehicle, crouched down on one knee?

Soldier It is.

Brother 1 Go on, our kid!

Lawyer And your weapon is at shoulder height. In the firing position?

Soldier Yes, that's right, Miss. I was returning fire. There were bursts of automatic fire, from the flats and from the barricades.

Lawyer You *returned* fire?

Soldier Yes. I only fired when I was fired at myself. It was simply self-defence.

Lawyer And would you say you shot anyone?

Soldier Difficult to say. We were in a firefight, you see. It's difficult for someone who was never in a firefight to really know what it's like, Miss. I returned fire and I only selected targets. Gunmen or nail bombers.

Lawyer You know that no weapons were found on any of the deceased or injured in that area?

Soldier I'm sorry, Miss. But you have to know. That's enemy territory, that is, Miss. They're all in it. No one knows what they got up to before we got to the bodies.

Daughter How can he say that, Daddy?

Father I knew I shouldn't have brought you! Ssssh!

Daughter But she's letting him away with it. Why doesn't she ask him how many shots he fired? And why were none of them'uns injured?

Father Ssssh!

Daughter Ask him that one. Go on. Why were none of yeez killed like my uncle?

Brother 1 Sit down, you.

Lawyer I think we should break for lunch now, my Lord.

Freeze. All wait, then exit in order: **Soldier**, **Lawyer**, **Brothers**, **Father** *and* **Daughter**.

Scenario 3
Lunch in a Nearby Pub

Waitress, Father, Daughter, Brother 1, Brother 2.

Waitress Everything all right?

Father Aye. Grand.

Daughter Could we have some red sauce, please?
(**Waitress** *smiles and leaves*.) They got away with it then.
They're getting away with it now. We shouldn't be over
here anyway.

Father I know that.

Brother 1 You think our kid'll be long more?

Brother 2 Naw. Nearly done I'd say.

Brother 1 He's going great. Really holding his own.
That bitch lawyer tried to trip him up.

Brother 2 She's a lawyer. That's her job.

Brother 1 Yeh, but she needs to get sorted about whose
side she's on. And someone needs to shut that Irish cow
up, too. Before I do.

Waitress You all right here, then?

Brother 2 Great.

Brother 1 Give us some red sauce, will ya?

Waitress You finished with that sauce there?

Daughter Aye, thanks. It's for them'uns isn't it?

Waitress (*Quizzically*.) Who? Yes, two lads over there. (*She walks away*.)

Daughter I'd give them nothing. See the way he shouted at me.

Father Look, just eat up so we can get out of here. I don't want any trouble.

Daughter *glares across*.

Brother 1 Anyway, they can't touch him. He was only doing his job. Defending his country. Should have given him a medal.

Daughter I know the medal I'd give him.

Father Sssssh!

Brother 2 Hurry up there. Session's starting again.

Brothers *eat up and leave*. **Father** *and* **Daughter** *eat up and leave*. **Waitress** *clears the tables, leaving the red sauce bottle*.

Scenario 4
Coming Out of Central Hall

Journalist 1, Journalist 2, Father, Daughter, Brother 1, Brother 2.

Journalists *hustle around the family, calling*.

Journalists Just a few words. Any comment? Just a moment of your time. Would you mind taking a few questions?

Journalist 1 Don't you think all the evidence has come out now?

Father What we heard today was only lies. Not evidence. If you want me…

Journalist 2 How do you react to the comment that far too much money has been spent on this Inquiry anyway?

Daughter You want us to put a price on…

Journalist 1 The soldier only fired in self-defence. Would you agree that the Inquiry seems to accept that?

Father But I don't. Where is the…

Journalist 2 Taxpayers can't be expected to fork out forever. It's been thirty years now. Surely it's over?

Daughter It might be over thirty years for you but for my daddy and all his …

Journalist 1 The Inquiry heard today that soldiers came under a hail of IRA gunfire. Should those IRA gunmen be brought before the Inquiry?

Father I think anybody who knows anything about…

Journalist 2 Wouldn't you agree that you and your families have played the victim for far too long? Isn't it time you moved on?

Daughter That's what we've been trying to do but if we can't get…

Journalist 1 What do you say to people who lost loved ones at the hands of the IRA? Shouldn't there be an Inquiry into killings by republican terrorists?

Father I know lots of people lost loved ones but my brother was killed by state forces and if….

Journalist 2 There have been calls for the immediate closure of the Inquiry. How long more do you see it lasting?

Brothers *stand and watch.* **Brother 1** *gives the fingers as they leave.*

Daughter As long as it takes for the truth to come out.

Journalists *leave.* **Father** *and* **Daughter** *stand together.*

_____

Nobody sleeps any more, because the great
wonder of manufacture is a tireless reptile
with no eyelids.

_____

Production Details 3

Socio-economic questions brought pressure on the Peace Process as it headed towards a positive political outcome. The huge transfer of manufacturing jobs eastwards out of Northern Ireland as globalisation took hold threatened political stability and is the focus of *The Recruiting Office*. The rise in young adult car death, seeming to point to a society in which the value placed on life had decreased, is dramatised in *Riders to the Road*. The sketches *The Anti-Sectarianism Cabaret* and *A Kick in the Stomach and A Kick in the Teeth* offer direct responses to sectarianism and racism in workplaces under the new, shared future.

The Recruiting Office was first produced by Sole Purpose Productions at The Playhouse, Derry Londonderry, on 23 April 2004. The director was Dave Duggan and the company was Patricia Byrne and Alan Wright. I acknowledge the influence of George Farquhar's plays in this dramatisation of two people coming for interview for a job in the IT sector. Who should get it?

Riders to the Road was first produced by Sole Purpose Productions at The Playhouse–St Columb's Hall, Derry Londonderry, on Friday 16 November 2007. The director was Dave Duggan, the Assistant Director was Steve Wakeley, the set painter was Richard Hughes, costume and props were by Helen Quigley, the technician was Martin McDonald and the stagehand was Francis Harkin. The company was Carmel McCafferty, Aoife Morrow, Catriona Simpson, Áine Fitzpatrick, Sean Canning and Kieran Pradeep. The play is a reworking of JM Synge's *Riders to the Sea*, with the family of the young men now facing the tragedy of road traffic death.

The Anti-Sectarianism Cabaret was first produced, under commission from Belfast City Council, by Sole Purpose Productions at Belfast City Hall on 19 October 2006, for a staff-training event. The director was Dave Duggan and the company was Judith Cornett and Alan Wright.

A Kick in the Stomach and A Kick in the Teeth was first produced, under commission from Derry City Council, by Sole Purpose Productions at the Causeway Hotel, Portrush, County Antrim, on 10 and 11 January 2006, for an anti-racism conference. The director was Dave Duggan and the company was Mel Lyle, Abby Oliveira, Dave Duggan and Jonathan Burgess.

The Recruiting Office

There is an office desk and one swivel chair. A sign on the desk says 'The Recruiting Office'. **Man** *and* **Woman** *enter at the same time, but from different sides. She is in her late forties, at least. He is in his early twenties. Both are in trouser suits (his is slightly 'odd') as for a job interview.*

Woman Where is he?

Man I don't know.

Woman They told me I would get it here.

Man Me, too.

Woman So what are we waiting for? There must be some pleasure amidst the pain.

She moves towards him.

Woman You're a fit strong man.

Man And you're a… fit strong woman. Fit for labour.

Woman Aye, but not yet. Work, yes. But not labour.

Man You mentioned pleasure. What can I do for you?

Woman Have a care. (*To audience.*) Men will promise anything beforehand.

Man I'm simply looking for work. To get on the job. Here, at the recruiting office.

Woman We're both only interested in the one thing. So let's get down to business.

Man Have you a trade?

Woman I had. Seamstress. Overlocker. Cuffer. Stitcher. I've done more than twenty years in the shirt factories. All closed. Have you a trade?

Man None. I'm a scholar.

Woman If you were not so well dressed, I would have taken you for a poet. Such soft hands.

Man I work in software. (*Beat, explaining.*) Computer code. Not verses.

Woman I worked in hardware. Hard-wearing shirts that women crafted and machined until the world had no use for us. (*Beat.*) You would use me?

Man As software becomes hardware, so it is with me.

Woman He's not here, then? Nobody is here, then?

Man (*Croaks.*) No.

Woman Then, shall I do you?

Man Yes.

Woman *pushes* **Man** *into the swivel chair.*

Woman Let's forget the preliminaries. No need for name, address, date of birth. I can see you're young. (*Beat.*) What is your star sign?

Man Gemini.

Woman Mine, too. The twins. Are we two, so alike, to be together?

Man We're going to be together?

Woman Do you know what our stars say? (*Beat.*) It's going to be quite a year. This is the year for trusting in your plans for the future.

Man I have made plans.

Woman A year in which you will turn your dreams into reality.

Man The stars say that?

Woman I read it in a book. 'Don't dismiss some of your ideas as being too far-fetched because you won't know what you're capable of achieving until you give it a try.'

Man Can you believe that?

Woman Of course. Fate has brought us to this.

Man I'm not so sure…

Woman Destiny. The Hand of Destiny is at work here.

Man I'm glad somebody's working.

Woman Oh! That's not all. You'll soon be working.

Man I hope so.

Woman I know so. (*Beat.*) We'll make it happen.

Man Here? At the recruiting office?

Woman Of course. (*Beat.*) No need to know what you like to do in your spare time or if you have any hobbies. Let's get to the core of the thing. You want a job, yet you say you're a scholar?

Man I have an MSc from the university. Informatics and telecommunications.

Woman Impressive. What has brought you here?

Man Hunger and ambition.

Woman The first I know about. The second I've never really understood. And what would you do to satisfy this hunger?

Man Anything.

Woman You would take any job he'd give you?

Man Beggars can't be choosers.

Woman Now you're a beggar. Something of a come-down from a scholar, I warrant. When did that happen?

Man Soon as I left the university. I have debts. I have a loan to repay.

Woman I'll grant you that.

Man Nothing more?

Woman You must be patient. If you are a beggar, then beg. What is it you want?

Man (*Onto knees.*) Please. I want… I want… I want… I want…

Woman Yes.

Man I want a job.

Woman Ah, yes. But do you deserve one?

Man I've studied. I've been good. I've kept my nose clean. I've kept quiet. I've bought all the things I was told to buy. I've lusted after all the things I was told to lust after. I've watched the films they told me to watch. I've dreamed the dreams they told me to dream. (*Beat.*) I've bought the suit.

Woman And you will do anything for this job?

Man Anything.

Woman You'll work in a sweatshop for low wages and undercut anybody else who works in the same way? You'll do anything he says?

Man Yes.

Woman You'll kill?

Man I never… I…

Woman You know what he does?

Man He brings jobs. He travels the world and he brings jobs here and we should be grateful that he would recruit us into those jobs.

Woman Grateful? (*Beat, dirty laugh.*) When he closed the last shirt factory and we all walked out, girls who became women in the place but who still called themselves 'girls', 'grateful' was not a word we used. (*Beat.*) Our hair gone grey in the place. Our hands gnarled in the place. Our eyes crinkled and lined in the place. The factory? It simply flew up and away. It simply took off to sunnier climes, where the hair is soft and jet black, where the eyes are unlined and clear, where the hands are brown and smooth. (*Beat.*) Where the wages are lower. (*Beat.*) Have you any idea what wage you'd accept for this job?

Man Enough. I only want enough. I can't make demands.

Woman You can't make demands! You're not a beggar. You're a slave.

Man You're no better than me.

Man *puts* **Woman** *in the seat.*

Man You're here, too. You want it as much as me.

Woman I want it more.

Man And you would do anything for it?

Woman No.

Man As you say, there is no need for preliminaries. We know where we stand. (*Beat.*) What qualifications do you have to work in the software sector?

Woman I did a course at the Women's Centre. An Advanced ECDL.

Man Pish.

Woman I have over twenty years' experience in the shirt factories. I was a union shop steward.

Man You're an agitator.

Woman I have agitated you.

Man I'll grant you that.

Woman (*Slightly mocking.*) Nothing more?

Man You were the one who counselled patience. (*Beat.*) I suppose it counts for something that you've worked before.

Woman For over twenty years.

Man You can't be that old.

Woman (*Dryly.*) I started in the shirt factory when I was four.

Man I've never even been inside a factory.

Woman It was hell. It was heaven.

Man Confused?

Woman Noisy. (*Calls.*) Clatter clatter clatter clatter clatter clatter clack. Clatter clatter clatter clatter clatter clatter clack.

Man *takes up the rhythm and beats it on the desk.*

Woman (*Sings and dances.*)
The clock on the wall says twenty to three
And that's where it stopped so we all could see.
The shirt factory girls, who sweat for their pay
Bent over machines at work everyday.

The shirt factory girls, 'tis true what they said
Held the city together with a twist of their thread.
The shirt factory girls, when all's said and done
Worked the day long to take home the mon'.

The shirt factory girls, they danced through the gate
Past cameras and press intent on their fate.
The factories flew off to sunnier climes
And left them to fend in more flexible times.

Man That was good. We should go into business together.

Woman (*Laughing.*) Aye, show business.

Man We got a good rhythm going there.

Woman We'd be wise not to depend simply on rhythm.

Man I don't think there'll be much singing in this place. (*Beat.*) Times have changed. No matter what you've done in the past, you won't be fit for the new technology.

Woman It's still machines, isn't it? Computers are machines. Phones are machines.

Man Yes.

Woman Well, I know machines. I know them intimately. I know the way they curl in on themselves, the way rubber sheaths metal, the way oil flows and grease oozes. The way levers clatter and armatures spin and spin. The way needles stitch and cross-hatch, bolts of cloth fly across stretching tables and all the great wonder of *man*ufacture is delivered by a crowd of women – girls – in noisy sheds as the sun slants across the dusty air and the clock on the wall sticks at twenty to three for ever. (*Clock-face gesture.*)

Man That is so old-fashioned. You have no idea what it's like now. Now it's all air conditioning and workstations, PCs and servers and monitors, laptops and headsets. It's all changed.

Woman Not all of it. It's still factories, just the modern version. It's still humans hunched over machines. It's still clocking on and clocking off and the clock on the wall is still stuck at twenty to three, only now it's twenty to three in the morning because they're wide awake all over the world and nobody sleeps any more because the great wonder of *man*ufacture is a tireless reptile with no eyelids.

Man And you're here for a job in it.

Woman I have no choice.

Man You're a beggar, too.

Woman It's come to this.

Man I never wanted to be a beggar.

Woman You wanted to be a poet?

Man You must be joking. I wanted to be… I… I… I was good at school.

Woman I believe you.

Man No, seriously, I was. I was good at school. I passed everything. I got all my exams. I wanted to be… I wanted to be… I wanted a job.

Woman Nothing more?

Man What else is there?

Woman *gets out of the chair.*

Woman Let's go back to basics. You mentioned hunger and ambition. Are you still hard enough for it?

Man I'm not sure.

Woman Let's see if we can stiffen your resolve. Let's look at this hunger.

Man I have no appetite for it.

Woman Don't give up so easily. We must have bread.

Man Yes.

Woman Food and drink. Clothes on our backs.

Man Even now?

Woman Patience. (*Beat.*) A roof over our heads. Something to put in the grate.

Man Or the oil burner.

Woman Something to put in the fridge. Something to light up the corner of the room so we can sit in the dark and be dazzled.

Man TV. Video. CD. DVD. Interactive. Satellite. Remote control.

Woman That's it.

Man What?

Woman Remote control.

Man You've lost me.

Woman Don't worry. I know how to find you. I know where it is. REMOTE, no. CONTROL, yes.

Man Take me under your control.

Woman That's the problem. We've beggared ourselves by letting ourselves be under *his* control. I know that sometimes, when the lights are low and the music is soulful and there is an empty bottle of rich red wine lying on the rug and the flames of the coals are licking the bare flesh of two delicious round…

Man Enough. How much can one man be expected to take?

Woman I know you're young. Sudden in passion. Quick on the draw. (*Beat.*) Patience. You must exercise control.

Man There you go with the 'control' again.

Woman You said it yourself. Remote control.

Woman *puts* **Man** *in the chair and pushes him back and forth.*

Woman You think you're in the driving seat, but someone else is behind the wheel. You think you know where you're going, but someone else drew up the maps. Someone else told you which maps you could look at. You think you're in charge, but someone else has control.

Man What are you on about? What has this got to do with hunger and ambition? I only came here for a job.

Woman You only came here for a job! Any job that he will give you? So, you will hand over control of your whole life to him?

Man It's the deal, isn't it?

Woman Maybe you should have been a poet.

Man Don't try to smart alec me. You gave over your whole life, too.

Man *puts* **Woman** *in the chair and pushes her around.*

Man
You went to the factory every day,
At the end of the week you collected your pay.
You've had a good life, brass in your pocket,
Rich of you now to be trying to knock it.

Woman Stick to the software.

Man I will. That's what I'm here for. And if that's what it takes to satisfy my hunger, all my hungers…

Woman All of them?

Man All my hungers. My hunger for food, shelter, light, heat, clothes, cars, holidays, spare cash to have a pint with my mates when I want to – normal things – the chance to meet someone and start a family, a house we could live in…

Woman And for that you're prepared to sell your soul?

Man You're making too much out of this. It's not a pact with the devil. It's only a job. It's a simple thing.

Woman If it's such a simple thing, then how come jobs are so hard to come by?

Man Duh, it's the economy, stupid.

Woman Don't 'duh' me! It's the stupid economy.

Man You want it, too.

Woman Badly. I want it badly.

Man Well, then, we'll just have to put up with certain things. That's the way the world is.

Woman But why should we have to beg? Is there no honour in this?

Man Honour? They taught me nothing about that at university. Look, face reality. You want to satisfy your hunger, all your hungers…

Woman Oh, but I do.

Man Well, then, here you are at the recruiting office and you know why you are here?

Woman You tell me, why don't you?

Man You're here because you're hungry and you want a job and this is where you'll get it.

Woman I certainly hope so.

Man And as we're living in the real world, in case you hadn't noticed, there is a price to pay.

Woman A catch?

Man If you like.

Woman Depends on who's doing the catching.

Man He is.

Woman But he's not here.

Man Oh, he's here all right. He's everywhere.

Woman Like God?

Man Not exactly. Not in the traditional sense anyway, but maybe in a new twenty-first century sense, yes, like a god. All over the world. Everywhere at the one time.

Woman Aha! Now I see. That's what made our factory take wings and fly. Up and away to cheap-labour land.

Man And that's why I went to university.

Woman You didn't go because you thought you might become a better person?

Man That's not what it was about.

Woman You didn't go in search of knowledge and truth?

Man No.

Woman Pity. (*Beat.*) That'll suit him, though. Do you know what he says?

Man What?

Woman Those who know the least obey the best.

Man (*Thinks.*) Now wait a minute, I did learn some things. Some home truths. Such as how to cook pot noodles and how to stuff two weeks of dirty washing into a small holdall and when to phone home to tap for money.

Woman Useful skills. For a scholar I suppose.

Man I know plenty. But all that's behind me now and I have to set out on my own. Earn my own money.

Woman How much?

Man Enough.

Woman How much is enough?

Man You tell me.

Woman I never really knew. All my years as a shop steward, there was always pay negotiations. I tried to get the girls to say what they wanted. 'A million a week. Get us a million a week.' That'd be the laugh. Nobody wanted that. We weren't crazy. We all knew the factory had to survive. Had to make a profit.

Man Makes the world go around.

Woman Makes the world go round, yes. Spins the wheel of fortune.

Man Round and round.

Woman Round and round until maybe it spins out of control. (*Beat.*) Did it ever strike you that when it was making its way around the world, it was leaving us behind?

Man How do you mean?

Woman Think about it. The shirt factories are flying off to sunnier climes. What's to stop these software jobs from doing that? Maybe not this minute, but someday soon. Someday when you've grown fatter satisfying your hungers and you have met someone and you've had the children. And don't you worry, I'm not for one minute assuming it will be with me. I know it will be someone younger, but just before that, you may be glad to learn a thing or two. (*Beat.*) From me. So that when you do meet that someone and you've got the kids and the car and the mortgage and he comes in to tell you that they're moving and there's nothing you can do about it and that it's all part of a normal society and that what you need to do is to get real, just remember these moments between us, this intimate chat, the way our desires and needs came together and he wasn't here to satisfy our most basic hunger.

Man Will I ever be satisfied?

Woman Maybe.

Man Are you ever satisfied?

Woman Sometimes. (*Beat.*) You also mentioned 'ambition'. A noble passion for a young man. I said I never really understood it. Strikes me you haven't any.

Man Oh yes I have. Ambition is something I have plenty of. I'm not going to let the grass grow under my feet. This is going to be my first job. But not my last. See, in this modern era you've got to be flexible, ready to move when the opportunity comes. Mobile in the face of changes in the global economic environment. That's why I got the qualifications. I'm mobile.

Woman Well, if you'd just stay put for one minute, you could tell me about your ambitions.

Man I want to be my own man. Eh, a woman could be the same. Only she'd get to be her own woman, if you see what I mean.

Woman Thanks for explaining that to me. And what will you be able to do when you're 'your own man'?

Man I don't know really. I'll just be free I suppose.

Woman Free? Working for him?

Man Well, I've got to work for somebody.

Woman But on what terms? (*Beat.*) Say he comes in here today, even though the way it's looking now that doesn't seem likely, but say he does come in today and he says, 'Right, you're on, here's your contract. Sign it.' What will you do?

Man What will I do? Why, I'll sign it.

Woman Will you even read it?

Man 'Course I'll read it. But I won't get too worried about it. It'll probably be just a standard thing anyway.

Woman A standard thing?

Man Yeh. A standard thing.

Woman Just because it's standard doesn't mean it's right. What about union membership, rates of pay, severance details, maternity and paternity leave, sick benefits, pension rights…

Man Give over, will you? If I start asking about them things I'll never get a job. (*Beat.*) Why are you here? Really.

Woman Same reason as you. I want to get into this software sector, too, but it makes sense to go in with your eyes wide open and that includes the eyes in the back of your head.

Man You're paranoid. You think everyone's out to get you.

Woman Well, I know he is.

Man You're very suspicious.

Woman Not really. Just very experienced.

Man Experienced? I'm not very.

Woman Didn't you learn anything at university? None of those nice bright young girls – or boys – offered you any experiences?

154

Man I was so busy studying, so busy staying on top of the lectures and the assignments; so busy staying on top of things…

Woman You like to be on top?

Man Yeh. Usually.

Woman I like to be on top. That might present us with a problem.

Man How?

Woman He likes to be on top, too.

Man Well, he takes the risk.

Woman But does he sweat?

Man I don't know.

Woman You will. And I will. And all the others who come into this place. We'll sweat buckets. And the air-conditioning will chill us and the clock on the wall will never even inch past twenty to three. Oh, we'll sweat all right.

Man I'm not afraid of sweat. I'm not afraid of anything.

Woman You're young.

Man I'm young. And I'm modern. That's the difference between you and me. I'm the future. You're the past.

Woman The past doesn't go away you know. And you turn your back on it at your peril. (*Beat*.) Your father and mother working?

Man Yes they are.

Woman And what did you learn from them?

Man What do you mean?

Woman I mean, what did you think when you saw them coming home tired and frazzled, then yawning and comatose in front of the TV; what did you think work would be like, then?

Man I thought it would be different for me. I'm not going to live like that. Heh, listen. Everybody gets tired.

Woman And stressed?

Man Yeh.

Woman And you think that's okay?

Man I think it's part of the deal. Look, my parents, they do all right. At least they both have jobs. And they have good holidays. And if they want to change the car they can. They even had enough money to put me and my sister through college.

Woman So you can join the same rat race, but only on a different level. Is that it?

Man I don't know where you get this attitude. My parents are not 'rats'. They're happy. They want the best for their children and they work for that. They want to see us getting on.

Woman Aye, getting on the merry-go-round. Getting on the wheel of fortune. Giving it a good old spin. You're tying yourself to the wheel.

Man You're tied to it already.

Woman I suppose I am.

Man Besides, my parents want the best for me and me sister. You don't even know them.

Woman I wasn't being disrespectful to your parents.

Man I know that. (*Beat.*) Do you seriously think it's not right for parents to want to educate their children?

Woman Will it make them happy?

Man Who knows? But at least they might be able to get a better job.

Woman Satisfy at least one hunger.

Man Many hungers.

Woman But only if he comes.

Man (*Beat.*) I think you should go.

Woman What?

Man Look, be reasonable. There's only so many jobs to go round. Not everyone can have one. You, well – you've had your day. Let me have mine.

Woman And what am I supposed to do?

Man Just let me have the job. You're too old.

Woman How old do you think I am?

Man Don't know. Nearly sixty?

Woman You're some pup! You really know the way to a girl's heart. Look, I'm older than you but I'm not 'nearly sixty'. And I'm not ready for the scrap heap. You need to wise up. People are living longer now and he knows that. Why should he go for a wee wean with no living behind him when he could have me, with years of experience behind me?

Man Because you'll only cause him bother. You'll only want to start a union and never stop complaining about tea breaks and holidays.

Woman And what's wrong with that? What kind of a place is he going to run if he won't allow a union?

Man You'll just want to come in here and take the job and not want to get ahead, because if you want to get ahead in a place like this you have to keep your nose clean and your head down.

Woman How can you possibly keep your nose clean when your head is so far down it's up his arse?

Man Oh, that's lovely, that is. That's lovely talk. That should really go down well at the interview.

Woman Doesn't look to me like there's going to be an interview.

Man There has to be. Otherwise what did I spend all that time studying at university for?

Woman Okay, then. I said I'd do you and I will.

Man What?

Woman I'll be him and you can be … eh… you.

Woman *sits behind the desk in interview pose.*

Man What are you playing at?

Woman You said you want an interview. You made it sound like a life-and-death issue. So. Here I am. Ready to interview you.

Man But you're… you're…

Woman A woman. Why thank you for noticing, sir. I'm in charge of Human Resources here, which is our modern term for… er… people. And I'd like to get this interview under way. You're not the only person looking for a job, you know. There's large-scale unemployment out there at the moment in case you hadn't noticed.

Man But where will I sit?

Woman You can stand. We can only afford one chair. Rationalisation, sir. (*Beat, mimes scanning a file.*) Now. It says here that you have an MSc in Informatics and Telecommunications.

Man That's correct. My Master's project was to enhance the interface between modalities of technological hardware and software applications in real-time infrastructural settings.

Woman Excellent. (*Beat.*) Can you make coffee? Handle a crèche?

Man I don't know…

Woman That's what we badly need around here. The place is coming down with software engineers and not one of us can make a decent cup of coffee or look after children.

Man I suppose…

Woman Are you flexible?

Man Yes, very.

Woman Good. (*Beat.*) Touch your toes.

Man What?

Woman Bend at the knees, slowly now. That's it. And touch your toes. Hold it. Now turn round. That's it. Stay in that position. Keep turning. Lovely. Perfect. Just making a note here. (*Writing.*) Memo 1. Get prices for tight-fitting slacks as uniform for all junior male employees. Eh… Memo 2. Introduce early-morning knee-bends and toe-touching throughout the plant.

Man Can I get up now? My back is getting…

Woman (*Coming round from back of desk.*) Of course, of course. Can't have you putting your back out. Not yet anyway.

Man Look. This is stupid. He wouldn't ask me to do that.

Woman He might. That, and a lot worse besides.

Man Well, you wouldn't do it. I doubt if you actually could.

Woman (*Bending and touching toes.*) See anything you fancy, sir?

Man You're just taking the mickey. Now in a real interview situation you would never…

Woman (*Returning to chair behind desk.*) Sorry, sorry. Just a bit of a giggle. Have to have a bit of a laugh at work every now and then. But we'll leave that to the one side for now, shall we? (*Beat, reading from file.*) Your qualifications are excellent, but what human qualities would you bring to this position?

Man Well, I'm honest and upright.

Woman Totally.

Man And I have real leadership qualities and potential. I was president of the Draughts Club at university.

Woman My, oh my! An athlete!

Man Well, I wouldn't… I am hard working and obedient, diligent and steadfast, an early riser and a good timekeeper. I'm fond of animals, especially fluffy cats and squirrels, and my earnest dream is for world peace.

Woman (*Reading from file.*) It says here that you are a member of the Revolutionary Anarchist Anti-Imperialist Armed Liberation Front.

Man (*Rushing around desk to look at file.*) It does not. That's not in my application. I was never a member of any…

Woman Just checking. We can't be too careful these

days. (*Beat.*) Have you any illnesses or allergies? Medical conditions or disabilities?

Man None. Fully fit.

Woman Excellent. Keeping in shape for all that draughts I suppose?

Man Yes.

Woman (*Making a note.*) Good physical vigour. Never give him the Intellectual Profile Analysis. Way below the threshold. Can't recognise irony. (*Beat.*) And you'd have no difficulty working shifts?

Man None whatsoever.

Woman Even though it plays hell with your family life?

Man Whatever it takes. Whatever the company wants.

Woman (*Closing file, breaking out of roles.*) Doesn't sound to me like the cry of a free and ambitious man.

Man Right, then. You're so experienced and you've done so much living, you tell me what I should do.

Woman I don't know what you should…

Man Exactly. You don't know. Except for one thing. You're in the same boat as me. Unemployed.

Woman That's true.

Man And if you go on like that, you'll not only be unemployed, you'll be unemployable.

Woman I have as much right to a job as you have.

Man You think so? Let me put it simply for you. Nobody – and that means nobody – has a *right* to a job. You might have been able to make that call when you started out, but nowadays there are no rights. Just necessities. Economic necessities. And your economic necessity… and mine… is to get a job.

Woman We could go into business ourselves. And I don't mean show business.

Man Have you flipped?

Woman It is an option. Everybody tells us we need more entrepreneurs. More people with 'get up and go'. I've got the get up. And the go.

Man (*Slight laugh.*) Where would we start?

Woman Right here and now.

She moves towards him.

Man I don't know. It seems so casual.

Woman Just the way he likes it. Casual labour. No contracts. No long-term commitments. Total freedom to do what he likes under the guise of necessity.

Man But what would we make?

Woman Software.

Man Are you crazy?

Woman What's the problem? I'm the brains. You're the beauty.

Man Who's the brawn?

Woman Do we need any? I thought these were the new knowledge-based industries. But you're right. Someone will have to sweat. (*Beat.*) Well, then, let it be both of us.

Man So we just set up and make software?

Woman It's a dirty job, but somebody's got to do it.

Man It might be worth considering. I have some project ideas. And we would get enterprise grants and advice from various agencies.

Woman Of course.

Man (*Excitedly.*) We could make guidance systems, targeting software, missile control programmes, defence shields, battlefield co-ordination protocols…

Woman Hello. Hello. Action Man! Calling Action Man!

Man What?

Woman Have you cracked? You want us to start World War Three?

Man What do you mean?

Woman When I said I thought we could start our own business I didn't mean developing an arsenal.

Man I'm not developing an arsenal. I'm developing software. I've got loads of material on this from the university.

Woman Oh, you do, do you? (*Beat.*) Let's get one thing straight, Action Man. I'm not interested in weapons. (*Beat.*) Well, that's not entirely true.

Man And what do you think he does?

Woman I don't really know. If I'm honest.

Man In the real world of business, you don't exclude the possibility of working in one of the world economy's greatest growth sectors.

Woman I suppose you learned that at university, too.

Man Actually I did. (*Beat.*) He wouldn't exclude anything.

Woman But I would. So, it's software for heart monitors, not bazookas; software for water purification, not jet bombers; software for dyslexia support, not cluster bombs.

Man That, too. We could do that, too. If it meant jobs. That's what you and me are here for at the end of that day.

Woman Everything's so bloody complicated these days. But that doesn't mean we shouldn't face it.

Man What's the use anyway? What would we use for capital? We'd need capital to start.

Woman We can capitalise this venture with our bodies, our minds and our hearts. (*Beat.*) Then there's always the banks.

Man Don't I know. They have me over a barrel already.

Woman It's not a barrel. It's a desk.

Man I know. His desk.

Woman Yes. His desk. (*Beat*.) You'd like to own it, wouldn't you? You want one just like it, maybe even bigger, with a glass top, or better still, a solid sheet of stainless steel, the ultimate cool, and a computer…

Man *moves round the desk, running his hands over it. He shakes his head.*

Man No, no computer, because this is an executive desk and an executive makes decisions while the computers are in another room being plied with data and information that are the knowledge you live by.

Man These are knowledge-based industries.

Woman Go on. Try it out. Go on. You know you want to.

Man *sits behind the desk and adopts a series of 'executive' poses.*

Woman That's it. Now you're getting into it.

Man (*On intercom*.) Janet. Cancel my two o'clock. I'm extending the lunch briefing with Tom Peters. It might last the afternoon.

Woman You've really got a knack for this.

Man (*On phone*.) Ah, hello, Tom…Yes, yes, we're still on… Of course… couldn't let a friend down… Ha ha ha. You've always been good at stealing my ideas… Ha ha ha ha…

Woman (*Janet voice, on phone.*) Sorry to bother you, sir, but there's an urgent call coming in from head office.

Man Sorry, Tom, just stay on the line a moment, please. There's another call coming in on line two. I'll just get them to hold. (*Beat.*) What is it, Janet?

Woman (*Janet voice, on phone.*) Head office, sir. They say it's urgent.

Man (*On phone.*) Sorry, Tom. I have to go. Someone else needing my time… ha ha ha… See you at one. At the links. (*On other line.*) Yes?

Woman You think it's all briefings and meetings, freshly ground coffee and brandy, black tie and golf links. But could you take the call when they phone about closure? Could you handle that call about redundancies?

Man (*On phone.*) But you said we wouldn't have to do this until after Christmas?

Woman Ah, but the FTSE…

Man (*On phone.*) I know we took a bit of a hammering on the Dow Jones.

Woman Yes. And in Hong Kong, too. We need to rationalise. You know that.

Man (*On phone.*) Of course. I accept that. We have to take the long view.

Woman For the good of the corporation.

Man (*On phone.*) For the good of the shareholders. After all, it's their money.

Woman Exactly. I'm glad you're being realistic. Seeing the necessities in all of this. Of course, you'll be able to access our new positions in China. Great opportunities there.

Man (*On phone.*) But my little girl has just started school. She's happy here.

Woman Be flexible, Man. Be modern. (*Beat.*) We're giving this to the papers overnight. (*Beat.*) Tell them immediately.

Man (*Hanging up.*) They didn't teach me anything about this at university.

Woman (*Indicating audience.*) Tell them now. There they are. The ones who sweat over the machines. Sure, you sweat, too. A more costly brand of sweat. Tell them.

Man (*Giving a speech.*) You know, from the last time I spoke to you... You know we... I mean the corporation... the company... well, trading conditions are very poor at present... you see the FTSE... (*Breaks out of role.*) I can't do this. (*Beat.*) You know so much, you do it.

Woman You think I haven't done it? You think I haven't stood in front of them and felt my words gather in my throat. Like crows. The blackest, darkest crows you have ever seen, that flew out of my mouth and cast their deep dark shadows over us all. Then led us out the factory doors, our heads bowed, the clanging of the gates ringing hell's bells in our ears. (*Beat.*) So, if you see yourself behind that desk someday, you'd better be ready to harden yourself, I mean really harden yourself, so that when you face that day, the words can fly out of your mouth like sweet reasonable reality and you can get someone else to mouth the crows.

Man Why do you have to be so pessimistic all the time? Can't you see the opportunities he's offering? It's not going to be like the old days. We're educated now and we can change things. We can make a difference. (*Finger pointing on desk.*) Right here and now.

Woman (*Scornfully.*) This is your ambition. This is the depth of it. A desk.

Man Not just a desk. It's not about the desk. It's about the position.

Woman On top?

Man Yes.

Woman So somebody has to be on the bottom?

Man You're being unrealistic again. (*Beat.*) Let's say he comes in now, and I accept that it looks like he won't be coming, but let's say he did, and he gave you a job, handed you the contract and all. You'd read it, of course. But would you sign it, then?

Woman Only if it met my terms and conditions.

Man Then you'll starve. You'll never get a job. You'll hunger and you'll waste away and all your experience and all your fine words will count for nothing.

Woman I said I didn't understand ambition. But now I realise I understand it only too well. I am ambitious for my rights. Rights that people like me and your parents have struggled for over the years. Rights that are always under threat unless we hold together, especially in these times of change.

169

Man What are your terms and conditions?

Woman Above all else I want my dignity.

Man (*Beat.*) So do I.

Woman Self-respect.

Man Of course.

Woman And self-esteem.

Man Essential.

Woman On those terms and conditions, I will seek to sell my labour. (*Beat.*) I will work for him. I will work for anybody. God knows, I've done enough of it down the years. But I will not be anybody's slave. Service but not servility. Those are my terms and conditions. Is that enough ambition for you?

Man (*Thinks.*) Dignity. (*Sings.*)
See me starting out
In the world of work.
See my heart ablaze
With my dreams and hopes.
I know that I must
Secure all my trust
With dignity.

As the clocks go round
And the profits rise,
See me hold my head,
With my friends, on high.
For no matter what
I'll secure my lot
With dignity.

Open up your hearts,
Let you spirits soar.
From the office desk
And the factory floor.
While the shop tills ring
You will hear us sing
With dignity.

Woman Whether you're behind the desk, in front of the desk, under the bloody desk…

Man Or on top of it?

Woman Patience indeed. (*Beat.*) Enough?

Man Enough.

Woman There is nobody coming, then?

Man Not just yet.

Woman And we are here all alone?

Man It's a golden opportunity for an experience.

Woman One not to be missed.

They turn the desk on its end and get behind it. They are partially visible, as they undress each other. She produces a pair of red boxers. He produces a red bra.

Man As you said, it's not so simple a matter.

Woman Finding a job is hard enough, getting on the job is harder still.

Man We need to co-operate.

Woman Unite. (*Beat.*) Are you ready? Prepared? Playing safe? (*She waves a condom.*)

Man Yes.

Woman Let's strike while the iron is hot!

Man It's bloody boiling!

Woman (*Loud zip noise. Beat.*) Hardware it is, then.

Man Hurry up, will ya!

Woman At least this way there's no question about who's on top.

They make love noisily and quickly. Then they re-appear, tousled and unkempt. Sated. They settle their clothes.

Man Are you all right?

Woman Yeh.

Man Now that was an experience.

Woman Welcome to the world of work.

They right the desk.

Man He didn't come, so he didn't?

Woman No. *He* didn't come.

Man (*Laughs.*) Thanks for the work experience.

Woman (*Smiles.*) Thank you. (*Beat.*) I'm glad I met you. I hope you do get a job.

Man I hope you do, too.

Woman You know a funny thing? You could end up as my supervisor or something.

Man Funny, isn't it? But it could happen.

Woman Then again, I might start my own business.

Man And maybe you could employ me.

Woman You know what? I think I will go into business on my own.

Man At least I know you'd do it right.

Woman Of course.

Man See when I do get a job, I'll make sure it's on the right terms and conditions. And I'll see about a union, too.

Woman Just so long as you remember this little time we've had.

Man I should tell you something. About the interview.

Woman Yeh?

Man I was never president of the University Draughts Club.

Woman You were taking the mickey?

Man Yeh.

Woman I thought so. I enjoyed it. That'll help you survive when you do get a job. (*Beat.*) Good luck.

Man Yeh. Good luck.

She leaves.

He leaves.

Riders to the Road

Scene 1

We see the kitchen / living room of a modern semi-rural bungalow.

Cathleen, *a young woman of about twenty, checks the pizza in the oven and begins to prepare a single place for a meal at the table.*

Nora, *a younger woman, puts her head in at the door to the yard.*

Nora Where is she?

Cathleen She's lying down. Maybe sleeping.

Nora *comes in with an official envelope in her hand.*

Cathleen What's that?

Nora The solicitor pulled up with it. I got it off him before he came in. (*Beat.*) It's the report of the crash.

Cathleen *stops setting the table and listens intently at the door to the rest of the house.*

Nora We can read it and see what it says about Michael. Before she looks at it.

Cathleen What can it say about Michael? Didn't we bury him?

Nora It can say how he died and maybe why he died,

and if that'll do her no good, we can say nothing about it. Till she stops killing herself with crying.

Cathleen (*Almost angry.*) Can the solicitor stop Bartley going to the auction in Belfast tonight?

Nora The solicitor can't stop him and she can't stop him, but she can tell him to stay inside the limits and to check the vehicle before he goes. He's her last son.

Cathleen (*Beat.*) Is the ice bad by the White Roundabout, Nora?

Nora Fairly bad. There's snow rolling in from the north and it'll be worse when the wind rises in the night.

She walks to the table with the envelope.

Will I open it now?

Cathleen Maybe she'll wake up and come in before we're finished.

Cathleen *comes to the table.*

Cathleen It won't be easy reading. She'll see the two of us crying.

Nora (*Goes to the inner door.*) She's moving about on the bed. She'll be coming in a minute.

Cathleen Give me the letter and I'll put it on top of the fridge. Maybe tomorrow, if she's stronger, we can face it.

Cathleen *hides the letter on top of the fridge.*

Scene 2

Maurya *enters from the inner room.*

Maurya Haven't ye ate enough this day already?

Cathleen I'm doing a pizza for Bartley. He'll need it if he hits the road for Belfast.

Maurya He won't go tonight with icy roads and the snow coming. He won't go. And if he does, I'll stop him.

Nora (*Beat.*) I heard Eamon Simon and Colin Hamilton and Stephen Donnelly saying he would go.

Maurya Where is he now?

Nora He went to see if anyone else was going. It won't be long until he's here. (*Beat.*) The gritter went up already. There's snow forecast.

We hear the sound of a car on gravel.

Cathleen I hear someone.

Nora (*Looking out.*) He's coming now and he's in a hurry.

Scene 3

Bartley *comes in from the yard. He is wearing* **Michael's** *fleece jacket under a motor car leather jacket. He is carrying a shock absorber, which he places on the table.*

Bartley Where's the keys of the red Audi Michael bought in Dublin?

Cathleen Give them to him, Nora. They're on the nail. I hung them up there because the dog had them on the floor.

Nora (*Passing him the keys*.) Is that them, Bartley?

Maurya You'd do right to leave them keys hanging there. They'll be wanted if we get any news of Michael tomorrow. Or the day after. We made a deep grave for him, but we must wait to know his state of rest.

Bartley (*Hefting the keys*.) I need the keys to take the Audi. I want to pull the grey trailer. This is the one auction for two weeks and they say it'll be a good auction for imports. I have to be quick.

He goes out, pausing at the door to look back. Then we hear a car start up and pull off across gravel.

Scene 4

Maurya He's gone now and we'll not see him again. He's gone now and when the black night falls I'll have no son left.

Cathleen Why wouldn't you wish him 'all the best' when he looked back at you from the door? Aren't we broken-hearted enough in this house without you sending him out with the cold shoulder and a hard word?

Maurya *takes up the TV remote control and channel surfs aimlessly, muttering at the screen, with the sound down low.*

Nora There's nothing on that thing.

Cathleen Ach, Nora, we forgot the pizza.

She goes to the cooker.

Nora He'll be famished out on the dark road. He ate nothing since morning.

Cathleen (*Slightly angry.*) He'll be famished all right. And me senseless to it. How can anyone have sense in this house with an old woman chattering forever?

Cathleen *takes a cooked pizza out of the oven.* **Maurya** *sways in her chair.* **Cathleen** *wraps the pizza in a tea towel.*

Cathleen (*To* **Maurya**.) You take the jeep and go down the farm road for a short cut and you'll meet him at the crossroads. You can take back the hard word. Give him this pizza and your best wishes on his way.

Maurya Will I make it?

Cathleen Go now. Quickly.

Maurya It's hard set I am to walk.

Cathleen Give her the keys. Just take it easy on the big stones.

Nora Which keys?

Cathleen The keys of the jeep Michael bought in Derry.

Nora *gets the keys from the nail on the wall.* **Maurya** *flicks off the TV and takes the keys from* **Nora**.

Maurya It used to be the old people would leave things for their sons and daughters, but nowadays it is the young men who are leaving things behind for us old ones.

Maurya *goes out slowly, putting on a scarf and a coat. We hear a jeep start up and pull off across gravel.*

Scene 5

Nora *goes to the fridge.*

Cathleen Wait, Nora. Maybe she'll come back. She's so far through that you wouldn't know what she'd do.

Nora Is she gone out of the yard?

Cathleen (*Looking out.*) She's gone now. Get the report while we have the chance.

Nora (*Getting the envelope from the top of the fridge.*) The solicitor said we could go and talk to him if we had any questions.

Cathleen (*Taking the letter.*) Did he say what way Michael was found?

Nora There were two witnesses, the solicitor said. They nearly ran into Michael on the dark road.

Cathleen (*Struggling to open the envelope.*) I need a knife, Nora. My fingers are trembling and there's a black knot in my stomach.

Nora *gives her a knife.*

180

Nora It's a long way from here to the north country. Where Michael was killed.

Cathleen It is, Nora. There was a dealer here last week who said it would be two days' hard driving to get there.

Nora I wonder how long our Michael took. And he flying.

Cathleen *opens the envelope, takes the solicitor's report and reads.*

Cathleen I can't bear to read it, Nora. It's hard to tell what really happened. And I'm cold reading it.

Nora Let me get you Michael's jacket. That good fleece one.

She looks through the jackets hanging by the keys.

It's not here with these, Cathleen. Where is it?

Cathleen I think Bartley put it on this morning. His own fleece was thick with sump oil. Give me that old one. It'll do.

Nora *brings her over an old jacket and drapes it round her.*

Cathleen (*Reading.*) It's the same old story, Nora. There's more of it every day all over the country with loads of other young men, not only our Michael.

Nora (*Taking the papers and reading.*) It's speed, Cathleen. It's speed. And what will she say when she reads this and our Bartley on the road now?

Cathleen It's the plain truth. A plain story.

Nora It's a plain story and one we've heard before, three and four and more times than enough.

Cathleen That's the number all right. More times than enough. (*Crying out.*) Ach, Nora, isn't it a bitter thing to think of Michael driving all that way and no one or no thing to guide him only the black crows that swoop along the roads.

Nora (*Throwing herself into a chair.*) And isn't it a pitiful thing when there is nothing left of a young man who was a great driver and a great mechanic but an old jacket and a bit of a plain story?

We hear a jeep coming over gravel. We hear the jeep parking and a door slamming.

Cathleen That's her, Nora. I hear the jeep pulling in.

Nora She's coming in the back door.

Cathleen Put this away before she sees it. Maybe she'll be easier after wishing Bartley well and we won't say anything about this while he's on the road.

Nora *takes the letter from* **Cathleen** *and puts it on top of the fridge again.* **Cathleen** *hangs up the jacket and goes to the table and clears the setting.*

Nora We'll put it here for now. Will she see I was crying?

Cathleen Keep your back to her.

Nora *sits beside the television, with her back to the door.*

Scene 6

Maurya *comes in very slowly and goes to her chair on the other side of the television. The pizza in the tea towel is still in her hand. The young women look at each other and* **Nora** *points to the package in* **Maurya's** *hands.*

Cathleen (*Clearing dishes.*) You didn't give him the pizza?

Maurya *begins to cry softly, without turning around.*

Cathleen Did you see him driving past?

Maurya *goes on crying.* **Cathleen** *grows a little impatient.*

Cathleen Wouldn't it be better for you to raise your voice and tell us what you saw, instead of just crying? Did you see Bartley?

Maurya (*In a quiet voice.*) My heart's broken this day.

Cathleen (*As before.*) Did you see Bartley? Did you talk to him?

Maurya I saw the fearfullest thing.

Cathleen Listen to yourself. He's driving to Belfast now. Driving the red Audi. And the grey trailer behind him.

Maurya *stands so that her coat and scarf fall from her showing her tossed hair.*

Maurya (*In a frightened voice.*) The grey trailer behind him.

Cathleen (*Coming to the television.*) What's wrong with you?

Maurya (*Speaking very slowly.*) I saw the fearfullest thing any person ever saw. Worse than Bríd Doherty seeing the dead man with the child in his arms.

Nora and **Cathleen** Uagh!

They crouch down in front of the old woman at the television.

Maurya I drove the farm road down to the crossroads and waited there. Then Bartley came along in the red Audi and the grey trailer behind him.

She puts up her hands as if to hide something from her eyes.

Maurya Tell me it's not so. Take these eyes from me!

Cathleen What did you see?

Maurya I saw Michael.

Cathleen (*Speaking softly.*) You did not, Mother. It wasn't Michael you saw because he died in the north country and we gave him a clean burial.

Maurya (*A little defiantly.*) I saw him. This very day. Bartley came flying in the red Audi and I tried to flash my lights to stop him, but my hands froze on the steering wheel and he went quickly by and I saw his face and he looked right at me but I could do nothing. I was crying. But when I looked again there was Michael beside him, with fine clothes on him and his hair neatly trimmed.

Cathleen (*Beginning to cry.*) We're destroyed. Destroyed from this day forward.

Nora Didn't the solicitor say Michael was killed in the north country?

Maurya It's little the likes of them know about the road. (*Beat.*) Bartley will be lost now and you can call in the undertaker and prepare for the funeral. Oh! I won't live after them. I've had a husband and a husband's father and two sons in this house, two fine men, though it was a hard birth I had with each one of them and they coming into the world. And some of them died sudden. Some of them survived to us a while, but they're gone now, the lot of them.

She pauses for a moment. The young women start, as if they hear something at the door.

Nora Did you hear that, Cathleen? Did you hear a noise in the yard?

Cathleen (*In a whisper.*) There's someone crying out by the crossroads.

Maurya (*Continues without hearing anything.*) There was Seamas and his father, lost in the dark night, broken and scattered in a red muck all over the road when the Escort turned over. I was sitting here with Bartley – a baby, lying on my two knees – and I saw two women coming in, lowering their heads and crying and not saying a word. I looked out then and there were men coming after them, holding a thing like a red car bonnet and blood and oil dripping out of it. Leaving a track to the door.

She pauses again with her hand stretched towards the door.

Scene 7

It opens and **Young Man** *and* **Young Woman** *come in.*
Young Woman *is carrying a bloodied motoring jacket.*
They stand by **Maurya**, *who continues, half in a dream.*

Maurya Is it Michael or what is it?

Cathleen Michael was killed in the north country and we
buried him in a deep grave, so how could he be here?

Maurya There are so many young men cruising and
roaming round the roads these days, how would ye know
if it was Michael or any other man? When a young man
is on the road with the wind blowing, it's hard for his
mother to know where he is.

Cathleen Michael is dead, Mother. (*Beat.*) The solicitor
left in the report.

She takes the envelope and gives it to **Maurya**, *who takes
it in her hand, standing up slowly.*

Nora (*Looks out, seeing a vision.*) I see a body in the
ditch and there's oil and blood dripping out of it, leaving
a red slimy track on the white snow.

Cathleen (*In a whisper to the young people who have
come in.*) Is it Bartley?

Young Woman It is.

Young Woman *lays the bloodied motoring jacket on the
shock absorber on the table and spreads it out.*

Cathleen What way was he killed?

Young Woman The grey trailer jackknifed and knocked him over the ditch. He was coming back this way.

Maurya He was coming to say goodbye to me.

Maurya *has gone over and knelt down at the head of the table. The young people are crying softly.* **Nora** *and* **Cathleen** *stand at the other end of the table.*

Maurya (*Raising her head and speaking as if she did not see the people around her.*) They're all gone now and there isn't anything more the road can do to me. I'll have no call now to be crying and moaning when the wind breaks from the north and you can hear the traffic roar in the east and roar in the west, making a great stir with the two noises hitting one upon the other. I'll have no call now to be going down, gritting and salting the lane in the dark nights after Halloween and I won't care what way the roads are when the other women are mourning.

She strokes the jacket.

It isn't that I haven't loved you, Bartley. It isn't that I haven't thought of you in the dark night till you wouldn't know what I was thinking; but it's a grand rest I'll have now and it's time I had it. It's a great rest I'll have now and great sleeping in the long nights after Halloween, even if it's only a bit of cold spud we have to eat and maybe a stinking takeaway.

Maurya *falls to her knees*.

Cathleen (*To* **Nora**.) We'll have to contact the undertaker.

Young Man (*Looking at the car jacket.*) Bartley'll want to be buried in that jacket.

Cathleen I don't know. His mother will have to think about that.

Young Man She knows all about it. The funerals she's had.

Maurya *stands up again very slowly and spreads out the pages of the solicitor's report on top of Bartley's jacket.*

Nora (*In a whisper to* **Cathleen**.) She's quiet now and easy. But the day Michael was killed, you could hear her crying out from here to the roundabout. She was fonder of Michael, and would anyone have thought that?

Cathleen (*Slowly and clearly.*) An old woman will soon grow tired of anything she does. She's been crying nine days now, making great sorrow in the house.

Maurya *lays her hands on Bartley's jacket.*

Maurya They're all together and the end is come. May we have pity on them. (*Bending her head.*) And may ye have pity on me, Nora, and may the road have pity on the lives of everyone living in the world.

Maurya *pauses and then continues as the crying rises from the others.*

Maurya Michael had a clean death in the north country. Bartley will have a fine funeral and a deep grave. What more can we want than that? No man can be living forever and we must be satisfied.

The young peoples' crying rises into a long, anguished 'no'. **Maurya** *drops to her knees. The lights fade.*

The Anti-Sectarianism Cabaret

A man and woman – in top hat, tails and a cane – dance on, singing the lyric below to the tune "Cabaret". *Using their costume as props, they drop into the scenes, as Sam and Pat, interspersed with the song.*

Sing.

How would we like it if, one day at work
Someone should call us names?

Work is a place to stop all this.
Don't join in sectarian games.

We're sat in our office when somebody calls
You're nothing but an Orange fool.

Work is a place to stop all this.
Don't join in sectarian games.

Office Scene

You were supposed to have this report on my desk first thing this morning, Sam.

I'm under pressure, Pat. I was in here until…

You're under pressure! How do you think I'm going to look in front of the committee this morning?

If you'd given me enough time…

Enough time! I knew I should have asked someone else instead of some useless Orange fool.

Heh! There's no call for that kind of language. You can drop that 'Orange' stuff. There's no place for that here.

Right. Look, I shouldn't have said that. I'm sorry. It's the pressure.

That's no excuse. We're all under pressure. Look, put this report on the second half of the agenda and I'll have it ready by the break.

Right. Yeh. Good. Thanks.

We're a team. Never forget that.

Sing.

But worse than the calling are the whispers and taunts
Behind backs and underhand.

Work is a place to stop all this.
Don't join in sectarian games.

We pull into the depot and there we see scrawled:
NO IRISH WE DON'T WANT SCUM.

Work is a place to stop all this.
Don't join in sectarian games.

Bin Collector Scene

Last run of the day, Sam. Great to be back in the depot.

Happy days, Pat! Heh! That's new. Fresh paint and all.

'No Irish. We don't want scum.' No matter how many times I see it, it still wears me down.

We'll paint it out. There's half a tin of emulsion in the depot. We can't have this stuff at work.

Sing.

How do we handle, as sometimes we may,
Sectarian abuse and taunts?

Work is a place to stop all this.
Don't join in sectarian games.

We sweep up the leaves and the park's looking great,
Does it matter if we're orange or green?

Work is a place to stop all this.
Don't join in sectarian games.

Parks Scene

Green leaves in the spring, Sam.

Orange leaves in the autumn, Pat.

Still us sweeping them up.

Aye, you're right. Park's looking great.

Down to us, kid. The team. Orange leaves. Green leaves. It's all down to us.

Bring up the wagon and we'll get red up here.

Time for a cuppa tay and a Jammie Dodger.

Sing.

And here's the chance
We've waited for.
Let's make a move
And work together.
Right this way
Our future's waiting.

We won't let the pressure get to us now.
Remember that we're a team.

Work is a place to play our part.
Don't join in sectarian games.

Leisure Centre Scene

Male changing rooms are empty, Pat.

Females rooms are empty, too, Sam. Time to head home.

Another good day at the poolside. Time for a drink?

Aye. Just one. I've me céilí class tonight.

Suits me. I've band practice. We should work up a wee
number together.

Why not? We're a bit of a duo here. You get the lights, Sam.

No bother, Pat. You get the doors.

Sing.

And here's the chance
We've waited for.
Let's make a move

And work together.
Right this way
Our future's waiting.

We won't let the pressure get to us now.
Remember that we're a team.

Work is a place to play our part.
Surely a place to play our part.
Work is a place to play our part.
Don't join in sectarian games.

A Kick in the Stomach and
A Kick in the Teeth

1. A Kick in the Stomach

Four actors appear and discuss what they plan to do as they pull on overalls.

It's a conference about racism.
No, it's about diversity.
It's about the workplace.
Let's do a racist attack.
No, better do the impact in the workplace, say the following day.
We'll come on first and youse come on then.
I'll be the victim.

They adopt roles and begin.

Woman 1 *and* **Man 1** *come on stage carrying exhibition boards.*

Woman 1 Where do they want this stuff?

Man 1 It's for the Diversity Exhibition. In the Mandela Suite.

Woman 1 I thought that was in the Clinton Suite.

Man 1 Naw, they changed it.

Woman 1 Why doesn't that surprise me? Who organises these conferences anyway?

Man 1 We do. Remember? That's our job. We're a small

business. Exhibition Services. The Council wants a conference. We service it. They pay us. We eat. Business.

Woman 1 Where's the other two?

Man 1 Reparking the van.

Man 2 *carries* **Woman 2** *onto stage. She is obviously in pain*.

Man 2 She just collapsed behind the van. She was guiding me back. She's sick or something. It's her stomach.

Woman 2 *calls for help in Ibo. Groans.*

Man 1 She can't get sick.

Man 2 She's pregnant. I bet you she's pregnant. They all do that. Come over here to have their weans.

Woman 1 Catch yourself on! (*To* **Woman 2**.) It's okay. Take it easy. It's okay.

Woman 2 (*Groans, calls in Ibo*.) My stomach.

Man 2 I told you not to employ her anyway. She's only over here to take our jobs.

Woman 1 She's not taking your job. She's doing the job you don't want to do any more. Or that the bosses can get done cheaper.

Man 1 If she's sick we'll just have to let her go.

Woman 1 What about sick pay? Has she a different contract from me? From him? Has she a contract at all? She's supposed to have a contract. We all are.

Woman 2 *groans, calls in Ibo.*

Woman 1 Anyway, she's not sick. She was kicked in the stomach on the way to the shop last night. She told me in the van coming up here.

Man 1 Why would someone kick her?

Man 2 Look at her. They're kicking them sorts of people all the time now. I'm not saying it's right. I'm just saying you shouldn't have employed her. Why did she come here anyway?

Woman 1 Did you ask your brother that question when he went to Boston?

Man 2 That's different. He's wh—

Woman 1 White.

Man 2 Aye, he is. She can hardly speak our language. (*To* **Man 1**.) Are we going to have to get interpreters now for all the new people you're going to employ?

Man 1 We're still working out a policy on that. Meanwhile, we have this conference to get up and running.

Woman 1 She's obviously injured. Maybe something's ruptured. She'll need to go to hospital.

Man 2 Take her to the one round our way. It's full of nurses just like her. She'll find someone to understand her, because I certainly can't.

Woman 1 It doesn't take much to understand that's she's in pain. And if you must know, she is a nurse herself. She should be working in that hospital, only the Health Board is taking ages to recognise her qualifications.

Man 1 Well, she's no use to us like that. (*To* **Woman 1**.) You take the van and get her to the hospital. And get back here as quick as you can. (*To* **Man 2**.) You and me can make a start with these boards.

Woman 1 *carries* **Woman 2** *off.* **Man 1** *and* **Man 2** *carry the boards off.*

Man 2 They're nothing but trouble, those people.

The actors de-role and take off their costumes as they comment on the sketch.

That went well.
Did we get everything in?
Need to work on the ending.
I wonder what they thought of it?

2. A Kick in the Teeth

Four actors appear and discuss what they plan to do.

You be the chair.
We're trying to set an agenda.
Yeh, someone's asking us to service a Diversity Festival.
The rest of us are members of the company.

The four go into a planning meeting about a forthcoming event they're servicing.

Man 1 Okay. Let's make a start on the agenda. I've got... dates, venues, transport, liaison, catering...

Man 2 Budget?

Man 1 Budget, schools element…

Woman 1 Translation?

Man 2 Translation?

Woman 1 Well, we can hardly run a community Festival of Diversity with everything in English.

Man 2 But there's nothing in the budget for that.

Woman 1 Anything for interpreters?

Man 1 The problem with interpreters is that they slow everything down.

Man 2 The way I look at it, the working language of the conference is English and that's that.

Man 1 We'll put it on the agenda. Languages.

Woman 1 We'll have to do more than that. What's the point of inviting the local Chinese population to the Festival if there's nothing in Chinese?

Man 2 They'll only be here for a bit at the start. Just so the photographers can get a shot of that lion… dragon… caterpillar… thing. (*Beat.*) We could get a Chinese restaurant to do the catering. They might do it for free. For the advertising, like.

Woman 2 Would you ask a white catering company to do it for free?

Man 1 We'll pay them. Whoever we get. (*Beat.*) Will the Festival go into schools?

Woman 1 We have to find out the Education Board's policy on that.

Man 2 What do we need another policy for? We have a policy for everything now.

Woman 1 These things have to be done right. You can't just launch into an anti-racism programme in schools without a policy first.

Man 2 But it's not anti-racism work. It's a Diversity Festival. Everyone's in favour of diversity. Right? Look at all the Poles and the Latvians working in that new hotel. That's good for diversity, isn't it?

Woman 2 But not everyone acts like they're really against racism.

Man 2 The great thing about racism is that it means we can forget about sectarianism. Sectarianism is so yesterday. Racism is the future. I don't mean racism is the future. I mean diversity is, in terms of money, fundraising.

Woman 1 How can you be so cynical?

Man 1 He's not being cynical. He's being realistic. The whole funding situation is up in a heap out there. We need any hook we can get.

Man 2 (*To* **Woman 2**.) That's why you were hired.

Woman 2 What do you mean?

Man 2 Because you're a… you're a… you know.

Woman 2 I'm a what?

Man 1 You're a valued member of this diverse and multicultural team. Now can we please get back to…

Man 2 You're a wo… a ni… a bla… a person of colour.

Woman 1 Close one there!

Man 2 And you're one, too!

Man 1 So, we have lots of experience to draw from in setting up this event. (*Beat*.) Is that it for the agenda?

Woman 1 When is it? Only we need to know if it clashes with the end of Ramadan.

Man 2 What's the big deal there?

Woman 1 Well, you wouldn't organise it for Christmas Day.

Man 2 But that's different.

Woman 1 Is it?

Man 1 Blast. I've left the brief in the office. I'll just nip up and get it. (*Exits*.)

Woman 1 I'll get my diary. It has the Muslim holiday dates in it. (*Exits*.)

Man 2 Lovely. Bail out. That's it. (*Beat*.) Nothing else for it so. I'll put the kettle on. (*Exits*.)

Woman 2 (*To audience.*) Did you ever feel you were on your own in this?

The actors de-role and take off their costumes as they comment on the sketch.

That went well.
Did we get everything in?
Need to work on the ending.
I wonder what they thought of it?

Reviews

The Shopper and the Boy

'The spectator experiences an unnerving jolt out of the usual passive role, suggesting that we should consider ourselves active agents of drama and history.'
Jane Tynan, *Fortnight*, 1997

'The triumph of Duggan's text and direction is that neither character is presented in an unsympathetic light. Both the housewife and marcher are seen as reasonable people, seeing truth in their inheritance.'
Ian Hill, *Belfast Newsletter*, 1998

'The play allowed the young people of our community to explore and experience the feelings that can only be felt by those concerned as they go through similar experiences.'
George Newell, Cultural Development Worker, Ballymacarrett Arts and Cultural Society, Belfast

Without the Walls

'This time Duggan's device is to use, effectively, the form of a classic Greek tragedy, and it works. A provocative showcase production.'
Ian Hill, *Belfast Newsletter*, 1998

'The performances were powerful and the dialogue style elegant and poetic. Characterisation was clear and the stage arrangements effective.'
Kevin McKeaveney, Community Relations Officer, North Down

'I liked the dramatic impact of well-chosen words expertly delivered.'
Audience member, Enniskillen, 1999

Waiting....

'*Waiting....* has deep resonances that remain in the mind long after it finishes. This is the kind of play that makes people think and its strongest suit is in showing how each of the protagonists can help each other to a deeper understanding of themselves, their beliefs and their lives.'
The British Theatre Guide, 2004

'Dave Duggan's forty-minute play conveys the pain at the heart of so many individual experiences in Northern Ireland. It doesn't offer answers, but, through playing games, ostensibly to while away the waiting, they [the characters] expose their respective pain to one another and, in so doing, plant a seed of hope without ever slipping into sentimentality.'
Morning Star, 2004

'*Waiting....* personalised the problems faced by communities trying to let go of old ways of thinking and connected with every member of the audience.'
Kate Wimpress, Arts Officer, Antrim Borough Council

'*Waiting....* was an excellent, emotive and relevant play and has had a profound effect on my consciousness.'
Political ex-prisoner, Glencree, County Wicklow

'*Waiting....* is an entertaining, thought-provoking piece, which exposed students in the US to the complexities of the situation in Ireland.'
Kat Kavanagh, Director of the Minor Latham Playhouse, Columbia University, New York

Scenes from an Inquiry

'The poetic reality of the text and authentic delivery
of the cast – combined with actual recordings and
poignantly simple visuals – made for a genuinely
memorable evening.'
James King, University of Ulster, Theatre Studies
Department (retired)

AH 6905

'A thrilling, well-produced piece of drama that left me
thinking for some time. Make a point of catching *AH
6905* – it has to be one of the best pieces of theatre I have
ever had the privilege of seeing.'
Catherine Spence, *Sunday Journal*, 2005

'Dave Duggan's script is full of interesting ideas about
the dangerous legacies of our national history.'
Sara Keating, *The Irish Times*, 2006

'The concept of having the truth of the Troubles buried in
Daniel's body as physical pain – which sometimes makes
him double over in agony – is novel and profound.'
Colman Higgins, www.fringereport.com, 2006

'I find Duggan's use of expressionistic techniques, music
and acting techniques, indirectly didactic methods and
elements, reminiscent of Artaud's theatre of cruelty, quite
fascinating in the context of truth recovery.'
Eva Urban, theatre academic, University College Dublin

'There is only one actor. There are few distractions.
Everything is kept very plain and simple. Everything, that
is, except the play itself.'
Eileen Walsh, *Daily Ireland*, 2005